AGAINST
ALL ODDS

AGAINST
ALL ODDS

Memoirs of Resilience, Determination,
and Luck Amidst Hardship for an African Girl
Child in Her Passionate Pursuit for Education

BETTY OGIEL RUBANGA

Library of Congress Control Number: 2017901922
ISBN: Hardcover   978-1-5245-8270-8
               Softcover   978-1-5245-8269-2
               eBook   978-1-5245-8268-5

Print information available on the last page.

Rev. date: 02/09/2017

To order additional copies of this book, contact:
Xlibris
1-888-795-4274
www.Xlibris.com
Orders@Xlibris.com
753703

CONTENTS

To the Society of the Sacred Heart:

As an alumna of the Religious of the Sacred Heart, I feel proud and indebted to you for the unfathomable love and care you showed me as a student in your schools, in Kangole Girls Senior Secondary School for my lower secondary school education and in St. Charles Lwanga Girls Training Center for my high school.

From my first encounter with the sisters and through their educational works, I remain convinced that these women live by what they say, inspired by the famous slogan of their foundress, St. Madeleine Sophie Barat, *"For the sake of one child, I would have founded the Society of the Sacred Heart."* Like their founding mother, the sisters made me that very special child and made me become what I am today.

This book is to inspire you to know that your labor of love is not in vain. I want to make sure that you know that. I also dedicate this book to the many lives that are under your care the world over right now. In due cause, hundreds of thousands of them will be able to say with Ray Boltz the following words:

> *Thank you, for giving to the Lord, I am a life that was changed,*
> *thank you for giving to the Lord, I am so glad you gave.*

Foreword by Professor Justin Epelu-Opio

The late Ghanaian scholar Dr. James Emmanuel Kwegyir-Aggrey is accredited to have said, *"If you educate a man, you educate an individual, but if you educate a woman, you educate a nation."* A few decades ago, educating a girl-child was not the priority of many cultures in Uganda and, indeed, in Africa. Yet the real people who suffer the consequences of lack of education are the children that these girls, who will soon become women, will bring forth. There are unimaginable odds those women, especially in the rural areas, go through as a result of illiteracy.

The book you are holding is a true life story of a girl-child who was orphaned and grew up in one of the most neglected areas of Uganda at that time: Karamoja. Her greatest dream was to get an education, but she had to go against so many heartbreaking obstacles to achieve that dream. Betty Ogiel grew up in a setting that is unknown to those in the urban backgrounds in a region then that was a no-go area for the non-natives.

The village girl from a remote village in Omukuny, Ongongoja, a subcounty in the Katakwi District, endured all the odds, and she managed to get to a university and, of all, Makerere University, the oldest and premier institution of higher learning in East Africa, let alone Africa and the world. Her story in her pursuit of education in Karamoja, one of the most marginalized regions, is captivating. It gives encouragement especially to those that have a vision to achieve something in life. The message is that giving up is never an option because there is always light at the end of the tunnel and a reward awaits those who persevere to the end of the journey.

Against all Odds is a book characterized by luck, resilience, and determination as the subtitle states. The author brings out clearly the ordeal she went through to gain an education in an environment that is not friendly to a girl-child, worse still for an orphan.

This book will inspire many parents especially in the rural areas where the girl-child is marginalized to give her equal opportunities in life just as the boy child. Betty is a role model not only at her home but also in all areas that she is known. She has proven that when a girl-child is treated equally like the boy child, she can even achieve beyond expectations.

I first met Betty in the year 2000 at Makerere University Kampala. By then, I was the university's deputy vice-chancellor when she sought help in regard to funding her education. When she narrated to me her life story, I was touched and decided to pay for her tuition until the end of her three-year course. I found her story to be so genuine, and at the same time, I felt pity for this young girl from Teso. I was convinced by her testimony and found it to be honest. In the subsequent years, Betty did not disappoint me in her studies; she completed her course with upper second-class honors bachelor's degree in social sciences.

In her writing this book, I am satisfied that the investment I put in her produced the return I expected and has given me the encouragement to even support more girls and encourage others to do the same. This book is a must read for all, especially those that are undergoing a similar circumstance that Betty went through. It is also a good tool for counselors, coaches, and motivational speakers because of its empowering content; and I highly recommend that you read this book and encourage others to do so.

Betty is one of the scores of destitute children, especially girls not biologically related to me, whom I have financially supported in one way or the other to see them succeed in their education. I am very proud of Betty, and I thank her for writing her life history so far. My message reaches out to all well-wishers and people of goodwill. Your smallest contribution to educate a child in any way will go a mighty, long way than you would have imagined yourself. Enjoy the reading. You are about to be inspired.

Professor Justin Epelu-Opio
Former Deputy Vice-Chancellor, Makerere University Kampala

Preface

Everybody has a story to tell. This is what makes the world we live in a unique and diverse one. Everybody has something that they care about and that they can devote their lives to. Our lives are shaped by where we have come from and in direct relation to where we are going and what we want to achieve.

In between what we desire and its realization, there are massive twists and turns, heartaches and heartbreaks, and unrivaled odds. This is the story with everyone, just that all these odds are unique to each person. The antidote to these odds is inside of each one of us, and when we face them, we are required to reach deep within and unearth our resilience, determination, and grit. Of course, we do get help from time to time from God and the angels that he sends our way, but I have come to learn that the help he sends is in response to our determination and the spirit of never giving up.

My story, set between 1978 and the year 2006, is written for the sole purpose of *inspiration* and *encouragement*. I intend to bring to light the fact that there are some internal strengths that individual human beings have been bequeathed with that can virtually trump any opposition that they face. From all the corners of the world, we do know that time and time again, when human beings with determination have faced insurmountable opposition to their lives, comfort, purpose, and pursuit, they have found strength from the invisible world both within them and also from above them (from the Divine) to break through.

My heart goes out to the girl-children all over the world who face trouble at every turn, being disadvantaged as compared to the boy children. This is not to say that my story of inspiration will not serve the boy child in any way. Rather, my intention is to inspire people from all walks of life who are facing critical opposition and odds in their lives as they wish to have a much-better life than that which they find themselves in with my personal story.

I also want to make sure that the message of educating the girl-child is echoed around the whole wide world. It is just a generation ago in my culture that the girl-child was never a priority in being educated. That is the culture in which I grew up in. My story shows how, despite all these odds that I faced, including being an orphan and destitute, I found strength to carry on with the greatest pursuit in my life: learning.

I most certainly would love to encourage hundreds of thousands of "angels" around the world—people who go out of their way to do random acts of kindness to other humans, not knowing that such acts have massive effects that can easily reverberate throughout eternity. My intention is to rally all of us to look around us, take a stock of what we have, and consider being a blessing to anyone around us who is deemed less fortunate. You are the extension of God's hands, his feet, his bank, and his voice here on earth. You don't need to be opulent and rich to make a difference; you just need to care.

Acknowledgments

This book has been a success not only because of my own efforts but also because of other people's contributions. First and foremost, I am grateful to God Almighty for giving me a second chance to life. He has kept me in a very good state of health and well-being that were necessary to complete this book.

I wish to express my sincere thanks to my coaches. Coach Phillip Kambe, I am extremely thankful and indebted to you for inspiring me to greatness. Your advice both on coaching as well as on my career has been priceless and has contributed to my career and personal growth. I praise God for the day I met you.

Coach Lawrence Namale, thank you for sharing your expertise, your sincere and valuable guidance, as well as your encouragement extended to me. You gave this book more value. Thank you for your willingness to work with me on this book and your cooperation at all times. Your advice both on coaching as well as on my career has been priceless and has contributed to my career and personal growth.

Sr. Susan Anyango, thank you for being a mother and for all your efforts in ensuring that I get an education. The motherly love you showed me is immeasurable and will never be matched. Your words of wisdom have played a key role in shaping the person I am today. I will always love you, and there will always be a special place for you in my heart.

To the Society of the Sacred Heart Sisters in Uganda for my education, thank you for mothering me and enabling my dream to come to pass through education. You gave me an opportunity to further my studies, an opportunity that many have longed for. You created a good environment for one to study, and the values you cherished have shaped me into the responsible person I am today.

To Professor Justin Epelu-Opio, you are an angel whom God strategically placed along my path for a purpose that you fulfilled as required. Thank you for foregoing a number of things that you could have spent your funds on for my sake. Thank you for being a father when I needed one at that time. You have played your fatherly role to date.

To Uncle Nicholas, for choosing me among the seven children and introducing me to the sweetness of education, I thank you. You planted a seed of learning in me that germinated and persevered to produce the expected result. You encouraged and guided me along the way, and you gave me the love that was necessary for the emotional development of a child. Thank you for your priceless advice.

To my current employer (at the writing of this book), Total Uganda Limited management, thank you for your help and support. You have given me a place to flourish in my career and have supported me in my professional development. Thank you for being the organization that fully supports and values their employees. To my colleagues at Total Uganda, thank you for the love and support you have accorded me, which have partly helped me grow to the person I am today.

To Ernst & Young, thank you for giving me a platform to discover my potential and build a career in human resource management. You imparted in me the values of professionalism and hard work in an office setting that have been crucial in my career growth. You took me on basing on my abilities and not looks and groomed me careerwise.

Ms. Sharon Akioto, thank you for being a true friend and sticking with me when I most needed you. I also thank my numerous friends whom I have not named here for standing with me during the hard times that resulted in the writing of this book. Thank you for the wise counsel, encouragement, and time you put in to make the world a better place.

I also thank the strangers who helped me along the way, especially the one who took us from the accident scene to Bugiri Hospital.

To my brothers, Sam and Peter, and my sisters, thank you for being there for me. Much as you did not have a lot, your sacrifices and contribution were very vital in the pursuit of my dream. May God bless you and prosper you in your endeavors. I love you.

To my dear husband, Mr. Rubanga Julius Abunga, the bravest man I ever met. You did not run away from a woman with multiple disabilities; you confronted it head-on and have stayed true to your vow. Thank you for supporting me in achieving my dream and for being in my destiny. Thank you for the tireless efforts you put in ensuring that I share my story to the world, in the book writing, in reading, and in editing overnight. You have had to literally tolerate my past and present and will be around to enjoy my future.

And last but not least, to my dear children, Ronald Icaarat, Hansel Maku, and Hanan Vudriko. You are all destined for greatness; you give me reason to work harder and smarter. You spice up my life. I love you, my children!

Endorsements

My heart goes out to my dearest noblewoman, Betty, and the book *Against All Odds* is one of those books that will shift your thinking, challenge your assumptions, stab you deep in your conscious, and then lift you up to an awakening of what is truly possible.

Betty's wit and grace and love and ability to tell an empowering story all shine through this book, and I am so glad the book is in your hands for you to read the story and live the journey as I have in the last few years that I have known Betty.

Betty is an amazing student of life and a resilient human being who makes everyone she meets reevaluate their excuses of not living up to their potential. Indeed this is against all odds, and you are in for a great journey. Enjoy, and then go live fully against any odds.

Coach Phill Kambe
www.intelligent-Performance.com

With a beautiful and passionate spirit, in her book *Against All Odds*, Betty Ogiel shows us the plight of a girl-child left fatherless at a very tender age and growing up with a mother in dire, abject poverty. With clarity, Betty shares how, by cultivating resilience and determination, one learns to live despite the internal and external obstacles and to emerge from all odds a successful professional. From the beginning to the end of her story, we see clearly the extraordinary determination and transformation in her evidence. This book represents a revolution in the way we may want to think of poverty and the girl-child's capacity for self-determination and compassionate love amid all odds. Surely, Betty Ogiel's spiritual autobiography charts for us a wise path of living with odd situations. As I draw upon decades of my experiences in education working with girl-children, she teaches us to harness intelligence awareness in ways that will profoundly help transform our cultural attitudes toward a girl-child education and to help them find the joy of living even in the hardest times in life.

Elizabeth Nakayiza, PhD, author of *Mindfulness for Educational Leadership in the 21st Century: Quest for Mindful Leadership in Education Reform in Uganda*
Dean, School of Education, University of Kisubi (Entebbe, Uganda)

Are you discouraged about your life? Are situations tough to bear? Or are you struggling with being content? If so, this book is an absorbing reading that says there is no such permanent situation! There is a god of impossibilities who is truly alive! Very inspirational!

Dr. Robinah Kulabako
Makerere University Kampala

Part 1

Amudat

Chapter 1

Possibilities

"There is this girl who stays with Teacher Nicholas. I think she is a great talent. I really have a good feeling about her. I think she can run, and we should give her a try. She is always running. If you send her, she will be running. I have never seen that girl walking." One of my primary school teachers said that to her colleagues one day.

I was oblivious of this conversation going on (and that is how sometimes life can be), not knowing that people were discussing matters related to my potential and my future while I was in my own world and not even thinking about that very thing in the remotest way—that is the aspect of life that shows us that we are all connected.

Let me give you an illustration that you will be well familiar with. Have you ever sat down and planned how to be a blessing to someone long before you even told them so? We call it surprises, but to God, it is a plan! Think of it this way: At the time that you are planning to do this, the target person, for the most part, has no idea what you are doing. As for you, your thinking will be that it is just a concept in your mind only, but you will be wrong. Chances are that you have been nudged by the invisible hand of the Divine to do this.

This is both good news and bad news for us. It is good news in that we are participating in the divine formula and bad news if we fail to respond to those subtle nudges of the Divine. I believe this is how God works—through people, regardless of their background and relationship with him. The key here is our response to that divine nudge. What seems oblivion

3

to the one that is to be blessed is actually in the highest grand plan of the Master Architect, who is carefully moving all the pieces of life to fit together and form a grand story, like the one you are reading today.

We have eyes to see, yet sometimes it takes the perception of someone else to see for us and unearth that which has been with us all the time. The interesting thing is that maybe, left on my own, I would never have discovered this wonderful natural gift that God gave me. The other paradox of life is that the things that really matter or make great changes are sometimes those indirect things, those that we may not have focused on. Sometimes, what we think is a foregone conclusion or something that we think may never change stuns us years later.

How in the world, for example, could a girl robbed by the death of her father grow to inspire hope throughout the whole world? How could the same girl, born in a family of seven, go to the highest level of education the whole clan had ever realized since the world began?

My life is a typical example of the running track at that primary school. The track is made up of red soil that has been trodden on and looks lifeless— there is not a single blade of grass on it. Anybody looking at the track will not see any hope for life on it. And that was the story of my life.

I grew up in Karamoja, one of the most marginalized regions in Uganda. At a very young age, there was no hope for me since I was born already faced with boundless impossibilities.

I have come to realize that when motivational speakers tell us that our lives are in our hands, that is just half the story. The truth is that all our lives are not just in our hands. There are many other players that are significant.

What I have realized, though, is that there is a common denominator to all men: *possibilities*. In 1865, when the great Abraham Lincoln was fighting to emancipate slaves from subjugation, nobody in the entire world at that time would even conceive the fact that the same marginalized black man could one day become the president of the United States. In the minds of nearly everyone, it was not only unheard of; it was also impossible. Yet possibility is not a function of what our minds can grasp. Possibility goes far beyond the finite thinking of a mortal human to the realms of the Divine. And my story of possibility lies not with man alone but also with the Divine.

Today, I am certain that if it wasn't for the presence of possibilities in my life, I would not have been able to go against all the odds that this life dared throw at me to be the person that I am today and indeed the person that I am becoming daily.

At the very moment that my teachers were talking about me, my passion in life of sports was elsewhere—netball. I loved the outdoors in school more than I did the classrooms. I loved to play, and netball was my favorite. You would be pleased to know that I pursued the sport to the highest of my capability. But as for running as a sport, I was not in on it. I did not know what I was sitting out on. They say that familiarity breeds contempt. You highly prize that which you do not have. Once you get it, it decreases in value considerably.

I did not know that I had a God-given talent in athletics although I was operating in it, as the teacher rightly observed. In fact, were it not for this very life-changing moment, I do not think my life might have taken the turn for the better. And at times, this is how God works. Where I am right now is a sum total of such direct and indirect involvement with people.

You see, my teacher on that small recommendation had no idea of the impact she was bringing in my life. She had no idea that at one point in time, I would sit down and immortalize her in my book of my memoirs. I believe that all she saw was potential, and she had the audacity enough to point it out and pursue it to the logical conclusion.

At that time, I was not participating in any school competitions. When that happened, it was my sixth year in primary school. I was in Primary 6. In fact, at the point that the teachers were having this conversation about me, I was at home working. What would a young girl in primary 6 be doing working? you might be asking yourself. That, my friend, is a story that we shall delve in shortly.

Although I cannot share the pains that other people on earth have gone through, I am sure that my life is a classic against-all-odds story. The incident that happened early on in my life was one of the earliest indications that "cream will always rise to the top, even if it is put in a basin." And so, on this wonderful day, the cream was just about to rise.

The teachers came looking for me at home. I stayed with Uncle Nicholas, who was also a teacher at the school. At that time, the school was set to participate in Annual District Athletics Competitions. We already had a team, and in the two hundred meters category, there was already a credible competitor that was set to represent the school. So in my first ever audition at athletics, I was pitted against this lady who was the best girl athlete in the school and who was the queen in this category and the one designated to represent the school at the district competition. Other girls competing in this category came from Kenya, Kapchorwa, and Sironko.

I still have a good recollection of the events as they unfolded that day. I was barefoot, and my youth could be seen among the competitors on trial that day. I was the youngest. I wore a dress, the same dress that I had worn for as long as I could remember. One dress worn daily for years. That was my athletics costume that day. I might not have realized the magnitude of what was happening in terms of the competition. I might not even have known that a team was being selected to go represent the school at the district level in Moroto. But in my mind, I remember seeing myself probably nervous.

As the sports teacher positioned us on the running track and gave us the instructions, I think I had a carefree attitude, quite oblivious of the weight of what we were doing that day.

"On your marks, get set, go!"

And as my knee was lifted off the red soil on the track when the teacher commanded, "Get set," I do not think I was prepared to see what would soon transpire. On command, I took off as swift as a swallow, and as I did, that was when it struck me—I was not struggling at all! I was actually keeping up with the big girls.

Today, I can say that that race was so symbolic to my life, if not prophetic. Many of us have hidden gifts and talents that will never be brought to the forefront unless they are put in motion. In fact, a portion of scripture says, *"The steps of a righteous man are ordered of God."* God does not order your legs; he orders your motion, your steps! So maybe we have been waiting on God while all this time he is waiting on us to get in motion.

After a portion of the race, I realized another thing—I was actually *better* than the rest of the girls! There is a certain feeling that comes when you are doing what you were born to do. I cannot explain it. That day, even as I stretched my unprepared legs and muscles and as I exerted my untrained body on that dusty and dry athletics track in Karamoja, I started feeling the pleasure of God and the joy of using what I had just discovered in split seconds to be a God-given gift. And ladies and gentlemen, nothing in this world compares to that place of purpose. That day, as a preteen, I had a glimpse of the glory of doing what I was born equipped to do.

I do not think I ever realized the prophetic enormousness of this race at that time. Swiftly but surely, I forged ahead and took the lead in the two-hundred-meter race, and a few seconds later, the race was over! As fate would have it, I not only won the race but also defeated the best girl in the whole school in that category! This was my very first time to compete, and

I was competing against the best. To my recollection, I was even younger than this girl.

Of course, my victory did not go well with this girl. She had been easily dislodged by an amateur who was, in fact, younger than her. She was so crestfallen and fell sick. That was how I got selected to represent the entire school at the district competitions in Moroto.

The teacher's supposition came to be true. I was a talented athlete. A barefoot, one-dress girl from Katakwi who was in Primary 6 would represent the school at the District Athletics Meeting against all her odds. This was in 1990.

Chapter 2

At the Epicenter of Odds

By 6:00 a.m., the sun is already out over Amudat. Its rays pierce through the crevices of the house, and many a man are already awake. Karamoja is generally a very hot and dry place. By midmorning, the sun is scorching hot, draining one's strength and sapping the vitality out, inviting one to laze around. But that was a luxury that I could not afford to have even as a young girl in all my years in that place. My life was divided between school and home, and at reasonable times, I could be required to go fetch water and firewood.

I don't quite remember much of my early childhood especially with my parents, more so with my father. He passed away when I was too young to understand anything. As much as I try hard to remember his face, his voice, and his physical features, nothing of substance ever seems to come to mind. I have no anchored memory of my relationship with him. I do not remember life with my dad, and I do not even have a picture of him in my mind. I do not know if I ever longed for him. Much of what I know about my father is based on stories that I have heard being told, either by my brothers and sisters or by my relatives.

A father is a source of security to his children; without one, a child's future is exposed to so many odds, especially if that child is a girl. Stories are that my father was a subparish chief. I was also told that he used to be a tough man but very kindhearted. For instance, he had an *askari* (security guard) to whom he allocated a piece of land, something that ended up haunting us later on. When my brother had grown up, he was not happy that the *askari* and his family had come to settle in that land. So he started a struggle to get it back.

Only heaven knows what difference Dad's presence in my life would have made. Yet one thing I also know is that one's purpose in life is so potent that it can overcome so many upheavals, whatever form and shape and size they may be. It seems to me that I was destined for greatness, and whether or not my father would die before I really got to know him was immaterial to this fact.

There are scores of world changers that I can name today who grew up missing the involvement of their parents. Les Brown has a very interesting story of adoption and being raised up by a single mother. These odds in his life did not prevent Les from becoming one of the most effective, most inspiring, and most powerful motivating speakers of all time. But if you had asked Les back then when the teachers were calling him mentally uneducable if he would achieve this feat, he, let alone the people in his life, would not have believed you. There are many people I know today who have lived in the remotest places on earth and are totally cut off from civilization by abject poverty. But despite those odds, they emerged as great beacons of hope to their worlds and to the world itself.

A family is a very critical part of the upbringing of a child. As a child, you are always secure in a family environment, and as long as you can eat and have fun, you have a great childhood. You do not get bogged down with the nitty-gritty of life's details, such as where food will come from the following day. And so, when my father passed away, I must have been around three years old.

I was born in Eastern Uganda, specifically in Omukuny Village in Ongongoja Subcounty in Katakwi District in the Teso Subregion. Our family was comprised of seven siblings: two boys and five girls. Overall, I am the fifth born, and among the girls, I am the third born. I love the number 3, and for me, it is strategic and prophetic, so it is interesting that I would be number 3 among the girls.

As we grew up, I also cannot remember a lot of details about my brothers and sisters. I also cannot remember the circumstances under which my father died. My mother was an uneducated peasant. She stayed at home and raised us kids. She tilled the land we had for subsistence produce to supplement what father would bring. A family of nine people is an averagely large family even in the rural environment. If we faced hardships early on, I might not have realized the extent of those hardships because of my age.

To me, it is such an unfortunate thing that there is so little to write home about my parents and my siblings in my early years of life. And that is just one of other great odds that one can face—living away from one's family at a young age. But I honestly think that there was an invisible hand that was directing my life in spite of the difficult circumstances of my birth and upbringing.

It is the tradition of the *Iteso* people to always take care of the children of the departed. Shortly after my dad passed away, we were distributed among his relatives. This is a move to help my mom alleviate the burden of raising seven children single-handedly. In our case, I do not know what criterion was used to distribute us among our relatives who would become our foster parents. I ended up being allocated to Uncle Nicholas, the last born in my dad's family. He had just completed his teacher training course and was set to start teaching in Karamoja. I have two uncles from my dad's side. He has two brothers and a sister. Incidentally, Uncle Nicholas, who took me (or was allocated to me by the clan), was also the third born among the boys. I don't even remember whether I had started school or not, but most likely, I had started schooling. The sister whom I follow and the brother whom she follows were allocated by the clan to my other uncle.

11

Again, my recollections of the move from Teso to Karamoja are not so clear. Yet after I had lost my dad at that young age, I did not have the opportunity to stay with my mother.

It is kind of sad again to note that a young girl was forced by circumstances to be separated from her loving mother. To date, I do not know what was going on in her mind as she saw me departing with Uncle Nicholas. I tend to think that she was happy that a relative was going to take care of me, something that would be a major burden to her if I stayed. But think of it for a minute. What are the chances of us giving away a young girl-child to be raised away from her mother? Such was my situation, and again, I must have been totally oblivious of what lay ahead of me.

I think I must have been excited to get a chance to travel, just like most kids are. I cannot remember making a fuss over it or even missing my home as I left. I cannot even remember the details of that journey to Amudat. Uncle Nicholas was not married then, and so I think the presupposition was that he was in a good position to take care of my needs, being a newly employed teacher. Four of my siblings stayed back with Mom.

As a testament to the degree of hardship that we were going through, all the four dropped out of school. In fact, as fate would have it, the other two who had been taken up by another uncle had the unfortunate experience of also dropping out of school and coming back home to Mom. As it turned out, they were severely mistreated at the hands of the other family to such an extent that they had to quit and run back home for safety. That is what any sane child could have done, especially if he or she knew the way back home.

Children who are not raised by their parents are at a very high risk, especially in poverty-stricken areas. They are abused, overworked, and brutally put down. In my estimation, not only are they severely beaten up at the slightest provocation, but they are also verbally abused. A child is very impressionable, and anything you say to him or her has potential of being taken at face value.

That is why I think Jesus Christ prescribed the most bizarre punishment (if not torture to death) for anyone who messes with the future of the children. He said that it would be better if a millstone is tied on their heads before they are thrown headlong into the river.

Children who are not being taken care of by the parents are exposed sometimes to irreparable damage. They face insurmountable odds as compared to the children of the foster family. That is not to say that all foster families are that bad. No. There are many foster families out there that are doing a wonderful job of raising children as if they were their very own. May God bless such families exceedingly.

To date, one of my sisters is holding a grudge against a cousin who once said, "We are not the ones who told your father to die!" They had been taken to stay with another relative.

As for me, I stayed with my uncle in Amudat, Karamoja. When he took me in, he had no children; he was just beginning his life. I saw him trying to have a stable marriage—literally trying. He tried at least three times. A wife would come and go. This happened twice till the third time, the one who came and stayed. She was the one I grew up calling mother, even when she was young and did not have a child.

I wasn't baptized by the time Uncle Nicholas took me to Karamoja. People only used to call me by my surname till someone, whom I do not remember, decided to call me by the name Betty. It was in high school in senior 4 that I decided to get baptized and keep the name.

I do not remember the emotions that I went through when I was leaving my mom since I was very young. However, I knew that my present "mom" was not my real mom because I remembered leaving my mom at home. I must have been excited, but I do not remember being sad about leaving my mom.

Either way, before I was picked, life was not all that rosy. We were originally from Katakwi, but because of the Karamojong invasion, we lost relatives, lost livestock, and lost other property again and again. For this cause, my father decided to buy land in Serere to move the family to safety from these invasions. By the time he passed on, he had transferred us to Serere; however, at his death, he was buried in Katakwi.

When I close my eyes, I can vaguely envision the house where we stayed. I remember we had one grass-thatched structure for all the nine of us. I had several catfights with my sisters, especially with the one I follow. We were also very creative back then. We could collect rugs and create clothes out of them. I guess the message went to my uncles in Katakwi of how we were suffering after Dad passed on. That was how a decision was made for our respective adoptions.

But we had other uncles from the sister of my grandfather. She got married to a rich man, and her kids were educated and lived in Serere. Some of them were already in Kampala. I had an uncle who was, by then, an undersecretary in the Ministry of Finance.

I remember one time they came and brought for us a bale of secondhand clothes. Each one of us kids had to pick a dress. I have a special attachment to this moment. I remember picking a navy-blue dress from that bale. I was thankful, excited, and happy. That dress, God bless it, covered me for years! It was the only dress I had, and even on the day my uncle picked me to take me to Karamoja, that was the dress I wore.

I did not have any spare clothes to carry that day. My movement to Amudat was not any bit ceremonial. There was no suitcase to carry anything, and if the suitcase were there, there would be nothing to put in it anyway. I wore my favorite dress for years before my uncle bought for me another one, only after he had been put on the spot by the neighbors in Amudat. The dress got torn, and in a spur of creativity, I cut it up, and it effectively became a skirt. Remember, I was still under ten years old at this point in time, so you can be sure that this child was already taking care of herself!

I know that children have to be taught to be responsible. There are some children in today's world who are being pampered way too much. There are children who leave high school and do not know how he or she can get home. That child has been used to being dropped and being picked up from school by the parents. At times, we may not blame these parents. Some of them have stories just like mine, and at some point, they swore that their beloved children would never have to go through the hardships that they faced. Believe me, I understand that completely well.

Today, I would never in a million years wish the life that I went through during my childhood for my own children, or for any other child out there for that matter. It would break my heart into a million pieces if my seven-year-old girl would have to fend for herself in getting clothes to cover her nakedness. This is the responsibility of an adult.

So anyway, my small invention that day was legendary in that in Karamoja, for quite a number of months (and I think for some years), I walked around topless. Maybe I managed to survive because of the hot weather conditions. If I lived in a cold mountainous region such as Kabale in Western Uganda, I would have died of pneumonia. So maybe all things work together for good anyway. Karamoja is on the map not only in Uganda but in the whole wide world as a disadvantaged place. In fact, many NGOs that come to Uganda will want to focus on social interventions of one kind or another toward Karamoja.

The place where one can find the poorest of the poor is easily Karamoja, especially several years ago as I was growing up. That region had been neglected, to say the least. It was underdeveloped and unpoliced. There was hardship in every corner, and smack in the middle of all that malaise was a topless young girl—the poorest of the poor. No father, no mother, no brothers and sisters, no homelife to write anything about, and to crown it all, no shoes and clothes to wear.

Paradoxically, I lived in a place of civilization, unlike what you would perceive in Karamoja. I was the poor among the rich of Karamoja. It literally took the urgent nudging and pestering of my neighbors for my uncle to buy me another dress. All I remember is that in all my primary school life, all the seven years of my primary schooling, I was barefoot and bare chested for the largest percentage of the time.

That one dress that I wore from Serere—again, God bless it—was an all-weather, all-season, everyday dress. Come rain or sunshine (literally), that dress would be my savior. Whether I was at school, in the classroom, or in the field playing or whether I was at home or fetching water or firewood, you could not miss my signature dress.

And that is why I still believe that the realm of possibility is not a function of what man's finite mind can see in a moment in time—because at that very moment, if you had asked a human being to nominate the people most likely to fail in life in general, the human being would have selected a team of people and I would have been their captain. At that very moment, there was no logical way that I could have linked my prosperity today to any proportion of the pain that I went through. Amazingly, when such things happen to us, we tend to adjust to them, and they will seemingly never bother us anymore. That is why it is possible to walk around topless for half your childhood and still survive it all.

Today, there are many people in this world who have lost hope. There are those whose stories, when told, will make mine seem like child's play. At the time of their pain, it may not make sense for me to tell them that there is hope. Our very minds cannot put together the notion of hope in some distant future against the insurmountable odds that we are facing at the present. All I can say is that there is no formula for hope. Hope is a force far beyond the comprehension and grasp of the human mind.

In fact, at times, hope operates in spite of the human mind. But if you think that walking around topless for years is the worst that I had faced in my childhood, you are mistaken. That was an easy thing. In fact, the dress, or lack of it, was negligible as compared to the pain, hunger, anguish, despair, and a mountain of odds that I faced on a daily basis in Amudat. Looking back, I am filled with mixed emotions.

Sometimes I wonder what would have happened to me if I had a "normal" life. Would I have been this resilient? Would I have been this sensitive and caring? Would I have been this generous in life? Would I have been this perceptive about the meaning of life? Would I have had a vision in life like I do today? At times, I feel like the odds I went through are a crown that I can proudly put on today, for you cannot tell my story and give it structure and shape without talking about my odds.

So later on, when my uncle relented to my neighbors' pestering, he bought me one flowered dress. In all my life, as a child, there was no single day that I ever wore shoes. The closest I came to putting on something on my feet was when I had an opportunity to go to senior 1 (secondary school). That was when my uncle bought for me slippers—not shoes, but slippers!

Chapter 3

A Glimpse of Karamoja

Amudat is not necessarily occupied by the Karamojong. Amudat is predominantly occupied by the Pokot, who are fewer as compared to the Karamojong. These two tribes could not see one another eye to eye. They would attack one another on occasions and have revenge raids. The whole region was generally very unsafe. Even to date, you wouldn't travel to Karamoja in as carefree a manner as you would travel to Soroti or Mbale or Fort Portal. But that is the environment under which I was raised, or let's say it is the environment in which I raised myself.

Getting out of Amudat was a pretty risky venture, bordering on playing or gambling with death. Many people, including missionaries, would be slaughtered through ambushes laid meticulously by the Karamojong warriors. As such, we were effectively locked up in Amudat and could not access the rest of the world. Chances of a car being ambushed were very high. They would even ambush, rob, and kill people in a missionary car. I am glad that that situation has changed today as compared to how it was those years.

My understanding is that the Karamojong are pastoralists. They believe that every cow belongs to them and no other tribe has a right to own cows other than them. The Karamojong also believe that cattle raiding is not a crime. When you go back to their history, there are several versions out there.

As I was growing up, this is the version of their story that I was taught: The Karamojong and the Iteso were one people at first. They migrated from

Bahr'el Ghazel, Abyssinia, now called Ethiopia. During the migration, the Karamojong were the ones who settled in Karamoja. It is believed that they were mostly the old men. However, the young men chose to continue their sojourn to look for a better place farther than Karamoja. The name *Karamojong* means "old man."

The name *Iteso* means "the grave, the dead body." So it is told that when the Karamojong (old men) stayed and could not continue the journey, the youth were reported to have teased them, saying, "Let us leave you old men here and let us continue."

Amojong means "an old (wo)man." *Ikar* means "tired." So the full translation would be "the tired old people." The tired old people who remained in Karamoja implored their youth, "You are going, but you will be killed. Let's just remain here."

However, it is said that the young people insisted and forged ahead with their journey, finally settling down in Teso. So the tired old men who stayed in Karamoja all along believed that "those kids who are gone are by now dead." *Ates* means "a dead person." I do not know how they now came to feud, but originally, they were together as one people.

The Iteso are both pastoralists and agriculturalists. The Karamojong are predominantly pastoralists, and to a large extent, many of them owned small firearms in those days. It is with these weapons that they would wreak havoc in the area and thus render the region generally hazardous not only for the inhabitants but also for the visitors.

Raiding was like a game to them. It was kind of like a way of life. They had spiritualists who gave them directions on when, where, and how to attack before they could carry out a raid. At times, they were under strict instructions on whom to hurt and whom not to hurt during those incursions. These invasions would also be necessitated by the scarcity of

19

food and supplies, given the general terrain of the region and the harsh weather conditions.

One day, Uncle Nicholas and I were traveling to Teso. It was one of those rare occasions that we had to travel because of a funeral back home. To say that the roads were out of order would be an understatement. In fact, it was this situation that gave the raiders an upper hand to ambush vehicles, kill the passengers, and loot everything. That day, were it not for the car in front of us, I believe we would have come under the attack of the Karamojong warriors. I know this because we happened to catch up with them just after they had been ambushed and a number of people had been killed. We were traveling in a small pickup. It is intriguing to note the brushes that I have had with death throughout my life. This near-death experience, if you will, was not the first, nor was it going to be the last in the course of my life. But thank God, at that time, I escaped through luck.

Back then, the only safest means of travel was through the bus. That was because it was one of the means that the tribe used to transport their foodstuff and also used for their travel. But even then, the raiders could shoot at it. To the raiders, there was a general understanding that the bus should not be attacked, but even that was at the whims of a raider's discretion.

One day, there was a warrior who shot at the bus and ran away. Later on that day, when he went back home, he found people mourning. Upon inquiring what happened, he was informed that his close relative was shot by a warrior while in the bus. It dawned on him with utter shock that it was him who had shot at the bus.

Immediately, after an ambush, the warriors would run away because they feared that army men would come. In fact, the police would not handle the warriors. In those days, it was the prerogative of the Ugandan army to deal with the threat of the Karamojong warriors. Prior to the National Resistance Movement (NRM) regime, the situation would be so dire, and the insecurity would be so rampant. It is only after the NRM regime came to power that this major threat that had plagued that region economically was brought into some semblance of control. I know this because I had lived there and had seen it firsthand.

Now back in Teso from where Uncle took me and where my mother and siblings were staying, we used to spend our nights regularly in the bushes and sleep out there. This was not for fun but for safety. Because of the constant fear of the raiders, we could not sleep in the house. The raiders would be marauding regularly nearly every night, seeking to kill, steal, and destroy. One night, my elder brother Peter survived death narrowly. The warriors came and entered the hut and shot indiscriminately at the boys who were sleeping in there—three of my cousins. Their blood flowed to where my brother was sleeping, and that was what saved him because they thought it was his blood.

Teso, mostly Katakwi, was in grave danger. In the evening, you would not want night to come; you would wish that the day would continue. Night and darkness were always associated with great danger and death. I am told, and can vaguely remember, that each evening, we would strip our hut bare of the meager possessions we had—pots, saucepans, and all—and hide with them in the bush. Then in the morning, we would take them back.

The raiders were greedy. Not only would they come for your cows, but at times, they would also target your household goods. Sometimes when they were frustrated, they would kill. You would be better off if the Karamojong warriors came to your house and found a cow or a goat; otherwise, you would face their fury. They would kill you without even thinking. Such was the environment under which we grew up.

Chapter 4

"Working" Up

As I slowly came to terms with the general conditions of life in Karamoja, I was also growing up fast, and so was my uncle's small family. His wife had blessed him with several children, and it was my responsibility to take care of them, never mind the fact that I was still a child myself. My life, like I have already said, revolved around home and school and studying and working.

The very first hurdle I had to overcome was the language barrier. I did not understand the local dialect as well as Swahili, which was commonly spoken in Amudat. Besides, lessons in class would also be taught partly in English. My greatest ambition at that young age was to be able to speak English fluently. I struggled with this desire for quite a while until I mastered all the necessary languages. I was a good Swahili and English speaker, and I also became quite conversant with the local dialect.

I think the very first step for immigrants acclimatizing to a new environment is to master the commonly spoken dialects as well as the ways of living. They say that if you go to Rome, you should do what the Romans do, and I must add that you must be willing to speak *Italiano*! All I am saying is that I got so immersed in the lifestyle in Karamoja that you would have thought I was born and bred there as a native.

The school where my uncle was teaching was being administered by the Catholic missionary commonly referred to as Comboni Sisters. They were a massive blessing to that school.

I lived with my uncle in the teacher's quarters, and that fact alone made life a little bit palatable for me. As long as the school was under the management of the sisters, we had free flowing water in the taps as well as electricity. Water was such a precious commodity in Karamoja. You might not understand the magnitude of having water in the taps until you ran out of it. The unfortunate thing about the school was that the sisters did not last there for long. I think something terrible happened there once. It was so bizarre that the sisters had to leave, and the school was effectively taken over by the government. I cannot recall what exactly happened to trigger their exodus, but my guess is that the school was one day raided by the warriors and a sister was harassed or killed.

At the quarters where we stayed, our neighbor was the head teacher of the school, and Uncle Nicholas was the second deputy head teacher. As long as the sisters were there, we had running water in the taps. But it reached a point where we had to fetch water from the river. Uncle could not do the fetching of the water; neither would my foster mom do it. That responsibility naturally fell on me. It was an added bonus to being the only big child in the family.

Fetching water in Karamoja was not child's play. The nearest place where we could get water was more than five kilometers away! So this meant that I had to cover more than ten kilometers daily for a single trip to fetch water! Obviously, that trip had to be maximized. You do not walk for ten kilometers and come back with a pint of water. I learned early that the more water I fetched in one trip, the lesser trips I had to make in the hot and scorching sun.

Probably my resilience was being cooked and nurtured then. Sometime back when I was a working adult, one person remarked that they wished they could clone me and have two of us in the organization.

I thought to myself that the cloning is easy, but they would probably miss a major part of the whole equation—which is the odds that the original me faced daily as a child growing up without parents in Amudat, Karamoja.

So in one trip, I used to carry three jerricans of water, each with a volume of ten liters. Now, how do you clone that? How do you photocopy a person that carried thirty liters of water over five kilometers in the hottest sun with a bonus of a baby on the back?

It was also my responsibility to look after Uncle's kids, and so on such trips, the baby would be the added weight. There was nothing I could do about this. I would carry two jerricans in both hands and balance one jerrican on my head. I tell you, it is an art. The jerrican on the head can dare not fall, for you will either lose water or hurt the baby. It was that precarious, and I had to balance it for five kilometers. But I was the best in the balancing act among the water-fetching procession. This happened over a long period, year in and out.

My uncle's baby is now an adult. I still remember them, and they remember me too. The most unfortunate thing about them is that they cannot continue with school! Imagine a teacher's child not completing school! That is the most ironic thing I have heard. But then again, it goes back to showing the kind of luck that I was experiencing. Life was cutting out people in my family slowly by slowly and curtailing their progress.

First off, all my siblings did not get the chance to continue with school. Then, so were Uncle's children. I am made to understand that Uncle Nicholas fell out with his wife. When this happened, he must have been terribly affected. I cannot begin to imagine the pain and despair that he went through. I had seen him diligently trying to have a stable marital life and homelife. Just at the time when he thought that he got his breakthrough, his marriage failed.

Fetching firewood and water was a major hustle. Sometimes the mission would provide us with a tractor to go fetch firewood. I remember I was splitting firewood one day and a snake came out! I ran for dear life laughing! Probably that was another brush with death, but with my talent in athletics, no serpent could catch me!

* * *

I know my uncle really loved me, but the same cannot be said about his wife. While at home, I did not have an opportunity to play. Uncle's wife would make me work all through the day. My "mother," as I called her then, would engage me. Apart from fetching water and firewood, I would be responsible for preparing all the meals in the house, both for the adults and for the children. That obviously means that the cleaning around the house and the washing of the utensils and the children's clothes were all up to me. You cannot expect a child to be as responsible as an adult, but that was the expectation of my mother. If I ever came short of that expectation, I would earn myself a very thorough beating.

Now, there is disciplining children, which has its place, but there is also beating children, which does not have its place either at home or in school. I do not think I did receive discipline from my foster mother, but I can tell you that I did get my beatings pretty good and often! This hurt me not just physically but also psychologically as well as emotionally. When someone beats you and exudes emotions of frustration (seemingly from being upset at your misdemeanors), exudes emotions of hate (the source or destination of which is not known), and also exudes emotions of fury, the resulting beating can only be equated to how a human will deal with a poisonous snake.

So my voice was silenced, my psyche subdued, and my future put in such potentially great oblivion. Part of the reason of the hatred my foster mother had was the favor that I got from Uncle Nicholas. So when there was a misunderstanding in their marriage, I became the punching bag. I was the de facto outlet of her pent-up frustrations, anger, revenge, and resentment. Any slight provocation would earn me my dosage of beating.

Those episodes, of course, were accompanied by toxic words that she would speak over me.

Now, friends, there are very many mothers out there who will not know any better. The way they were raised is projected to the way they will raise their own kids. In addition to that, the scourge of poverty can really bring the worst out of people. It is very easy to tell your child "Go to your room" as a form of punishment when all your bills have been paid. It is another thing to be poor and have your frustrations compounded with the messes of a child, which are common and daily. I am willing to bet that if my foster mother grew up in a better family and led a good life, chances are that she would have been more considerate of me. Unfortunately, we may not be able to find out about that.

One day, Uncle Nicholas caught her in the act of beating me up as he made an unscheduled stop at home from school. That sight must have pricked his heart so bad. I think that in a matter of a split second, his brain could replay that sight happening to me countless times, and what bothered him was that he had no idea of those beatings taking place.

He was not amused, and he retaliated by beating her back and giving her a stern warning not to mistreat me. That day, I came to affirm the love that Uncle had for me. He later on did confess that a child in my situation needs constant care and checking up by the foster parent—in that case, himself. Of course, after he beat his wife up, she also found a way of getting back at me—she threatened me not to tell him anything, or I would keep getting the beatings.

Either way, the beatings kept coming, and I dared not report her to Uncle Nicholas. And that is why I still do insist that my life has never fully been in my hands. There has been a strong divine influence in my outcome, and I have this belief that the best is still yet to come for me. How a young girl was robbed of her father and mother and the rest of the family and transported by life to the most disadvantaged place in the country and came out as a beacon of hope is not an everyday tale. No, I believe this is an exceptional story.

Of course, I cannot even start comparing my predicament with others'. It is folly. Everyone has a story, and everyone has a song. But in each of those stories, I am aware that we can never rule out the play of hardships and setbacks. We can only paint a beautiful story when we start showcasing the finer aspects of the deliverance from all the odds that we faced.

My trouble is not the same as that of someone else, but my trouble is personal. It affects my personal heart. It affects my emotions. It dampens my hopes and causes me to dump my desires as if they are unwanted luxuries.

During wars, one of the tactics that an enemy army uses over the captured foe is physical torture. It is aimed at making your life uncomfortable and unbearable in a bid to break your resolve and spirit. Another tactic is verbal abuse and a barrage of negative news from the front line, supposedly about how your army is losing. That is exactly what very many children are going through around the world. My heart really goes out to them. Sometimes the things that I see people do to others convince me that they must be orchestrated by evil incarnate! There is just no other way that you can fully explain it.

My understanding of spiritual dynamics is that great suffering is a precursor of great deliverance. Probably many people who are seeing many odds in their lives are marked for greatness. In fact, I dare say that odds are the greatest breeding grounds for greatness. The late Dr. Myles Munroe once made a very powerful statement. He said, *"You never grow in good times. Pressure is the incubator for progress."* I must quickly add, however, that without the help of the Divine, I cannot see any way a subdued child, let alone a man, can come out of the doldrums and inspire others to be better.

My foster mother's beatings scared me daily. Her words cut into me like a dagger over and over again. Her presence in the house was pure terror to me. And this lasted for years. Were it not for the small glimmer of hope of the regard and care that Uncle Nicholas had for me, I might have been totally subdued.

Chapter 5

Early Schooling

In my "mother's" regime, as early as I can remember, my day would start as early as 6:00 a.m. It was already full, and my calendar totally overbooked the moment I opened my eyes. Of course, there was no time to change clothes; thank God for the single multipurpose dress I owned.

The first order of business would be to clean the house and organize it. Then I would clean all the utensils before proceeding to fix breakfast for the family. Remember, the cooking would be done using firewood. Breakfast would be prepared twice—tea for the adults and porridge for the kids. Sometimes I would have to make *mandazi* (doughnuts) for breakfast.

Immediately, after breakfast was fixed, my thoughts would go straight away to how and what I would prepare for lunch, but that was not to be done before I could bathe the kids and prepare them for school. This was like a full-time homemaking job that I did daily like clockwork. As a result, my own schooling was affected. I would most definitely get to class late most of the time. Of course, by the time I got to school, I was already tired, needing a serious nap to recuperate. But a serious nap was not what awaited me at school. Every time I came late and missed assembly, I had to be caned.

It seemed to me like life really did not care what I went through; things must proceed as needed. It seemed to me like nobody took note of my existence. Nobody *really* cared for me as a child needing care and attention. Love and tenderness from parents were something I never knew.

In order to escape the caning and to lessen my burden on earth as a child, I figured that the best thing to do would be to wake up very early. This could create ample time for me to go through the motions of my duties on earth and perhaps get to school on time. At lunchtime, I had to be disciplined too. I had to rush back home to prepare lunch. This had to be done at a supersonic speed and with a strict adherence to time just like the buses in Europe so I could be back for afternoon classes on time. Of course, occasionally, I got back to school late, as you might have guessed, because I operated an analogue life that needed digital precision. After school, when other children could go for games, my task was to go home to start preparing for supper, wash utensils, bathe the children, fix tea for Uncle, and do a couple of other tasks that needed to be taken care of.

My foster mother's enterprise was mainly brewing and selling illicit local brew, *malwa*. On weekends, brewing *waragi* (local gin) was also on the menu of my many chores. The brewing was an intricate process, and even though I cannot remember the right quantities we used to make a perfect brew, today the idea or concept is still in my mind. I was mentored and coached into that business. The processing was one thing. But then after you had processed your brew successfully, you also needed to master the art of selling it. You needed to station yourself in a good location, and you also needed to make good customer relations to keep the business flowing. I was coached in all that. The amount of money you would make from your brew would be dependent on how good your brew was.

Brewing waragi was a very common business in rural Karamoja. As early as 6:30 a.m., you could get customers who wanted to consume the brew. Incidentally, I did not fall in the trap of taking waragi. I could taste it, but it was not something I would enjoy. And this also, I must add, looks like the hand of the Divine orchestrating my future. I was smack in the middle of a bog that would effectively sink my career. However, like Peter walking on the water, I precariously survived the lure and the hook of the brew.

Waragi has destroyed the lives and livelihoods of very many young men and women and their families too. The worst is when you get hooked on it. It is so difficult to untangle yourself. And this is what expert brewers prey on. Once you are hooked on it, the brewer knows that you are under his mercies. You can sell your property just to get a sip of malwa or waragi. It then seems like the brew becomes like your oxygen in that you cannot operate without it. And I was right there smack in the middle of it, but I survived its hook. It tasted so bad in my mouth that I wondered why people loved it.

Had I fallen into that trap of loving to take local brew, I am not so sure I would have made it this far. Our lives, you see, are shaped in those precarious moments of black and white occasionally. Sometimes, it is kind of like a line of code in a computer program that caters to only two options. If you take option 1, there are consequences. If you take option 2, there are also consequences. To date, I really wonder what would have happened to me had I not been separated from my family. Although the most preferred way of living is to be with your parents, it turns out that had I not gone with Uncle Nicholas, chances are that I would have ended up uneducated just like most of my brothers and sisters and married off at a tender age like so many rural girls.

That interlude, however bizarre it might have seemed, actually did shape my life. The greatest extent of who I am today was shaped and molded in Amudat, Karamoja. And while there, the rest of my life was shaped by one seemingly isolated decision not to consume waragi that was readily available to me.

Of course, the process of making the waragi is rather tedious. We would begin by fermenting cassava or maize and sorghum or millet. Then, there was that unenviable task of fetching water—a lot of water, drums and drums of water from the borehole quite a distance away. Boreholes could also reach a point when they would dry. That was when we used to go to the river more than five kilometers away.

31

* * *

The interest Uncle Nicholas put in my schooling is to be lauded. Were it not for this foundation I got in school, my life would have taken a totally different tangent. Today, I hear very many people blaming the school system for this and for that. Not so many people want to give it credit for some of what it has done. What I think is that if you approach the education system as if it were a silver bullet to solve all of society's problems, you will be very disappointed.

I think another school that I was already enrolled in right from birth was the University of Life. From here, I learned so many things that I would never be effectively taught by theory in school. I learned through toil, experience, determination, persistence, hoping against hope, and basically building in me a great element of grit. Angela Lee Duckworth gave an impassioned talk on Ted.com entitled "Grit" sometime back in which she said the following, and I agree totally with her because that is exactly what I was learning in the University of Life:

> *We partnered with private companies, asking, which of these salespeople is going to keep their jobs? And who's going to earn the most money? In all those very different contexts one characteristic emerged as a significant predictor of success. And it wasn't social intelligence. It wasn't good looks, physical health, and it wasn't IQ. It was Grit.*
>
> *Grit is passion and perseverance for very long term goals. Grit is having stamina. Grit is sticking with your future, day in, day out, not just for the week, not just for the month, but for years, and working really hard to make that future a reality. Grit is living life like it's a marathon, not a sprint.*

So you could say that long before Angela Lee Duckworth "discovered" grit, I was already being trained at it in the University of Life.

My traditional schooling started immediately when I got into Karamoja in 1985. As I had already explained, I was green, I did not know anything, and worst of all, I did not know how to express myself in the local dialect. English and Swahili were predominantly used as languages of choice in teaching. It is safe to say that I was like a deer in the headlights in those early days of school. Of course, there was a special "accelerator" course for those who did not decipher English and Swahili; I had to learn this on my own and by sheer determination. That was just one of the odds I faced at school.

Another major problem right from the beginning of my schooling to the very end of it was school fees. In primary school, I was able to see my education through by virtue of a bursary I got from Christian Child Fund (CCF). All the teachers in the school were given an opportunity to have their own children benefit from this fund. Since I was the only one under the care of Uncle Nicholas at that time, it was only natural that he would enroll me in the scheme, something that I am forever grateful for. And that is another thing that I would like to talk about shortly.

There are many organizations in the world that are trying to make a positive social impact in myriad ways. CCF, United Nations Children's Fund (UNICEF), United States Agency for International Development (USAID), Habitat for Humanity, Society of the Sacred Heart Education, and so on are just some of those. I know to some extent that their work is filled with lots of statistics: how many children were helped, the ratio of girl-children to boy children, teenage pregnancies, and so on.

These are mere statistics. Yet behind it all, there are real lives of positive change that I am sure most have not been documented and showcased. CCF might have helped me for a term or two or for years, and they might have easily forgotten about it. But again, let me say this: if it was not for their intervention early on in my life, even as they saw me as a mere statistic, chances are that I would not have made it. I would have dropped out of school, and most probably, my future and the future of my children would have been aborted.

The same message can be said of those school administrators and owners who, at several times in different ways, contribute to the education of children of strangers at their very own expense. When they are doing this, at times, they may not know the impact of what their gesture will cause. That impact has the potential to reverberate throughout eternity. And so, at this point in time, I would like to take some time and encourage all the benefactors, all parents and guardians, and all nonprofit organizations that are impacting people's lives in different ways. I am convinced that there is no reward great enough and suitable enough for you here on earth. I am convinced that when all is said and done, your reward awaits you in heaven, so make sure you get there.

Despite all the odds I was facing so far, one thing was clear: I was a very gifted and bright pupil. I still am. That was what helped me. I started from P1, but I never completed it. Without prior education, they must have found out that I was way above that grade, so I was pushed to P2. I do not know how I performed in P2 going to P3, but in P3, there was a very tough teacher. I think I did not know how to read, and that teacher was so tough on me. At some point, because of the toughness of the teacher, I decided to go back to P2. Nobody noticed, not even my uncle, up until one day when we bumped into each other at school.

I was out of class with the P2 kids at that time, and the P3 kids were in session. Uncle asked me, "Why are you out?" I told him, "For us in P2, we do not go for afternoon classes." He retorted, "Who told you that you are in P2? You are supposed to be in P3." He took me back to that teacher and told her to always make sure that I was in class. (This very tough teacher, it turns out, was the one who later identified my gift and talent in athletics.) From there, however, I picked up academic steam like a locomotive.

I was always among the first three students, either number 1 or 2. There was a child who was my greatest competitor, and we sat together at one desk. People used to think that we shared answers, but it was not the case. They separated us. But still it happened as always: the two of us would always alternate topping the class, and it was so all the way up to P7. This girl was the daughter of the tough teacher I encountered back in P3.

I think competition is a very good thing for it keeps you on your toes. However, just the two of us competing for whole five or so years tells you the story of the quality of education in Karamoja in those days. In Karamoja, the overall levels of performance were quite low. I remember that a girl attained a score of 22 aggregate, but we were still the best at school. I scored 24.

As much as our primary school was a first-class school by many standards, majority of the teachers at that school were of low quality. Again, it goes back to the issue of insecurity in the region. Which sane teacher of quality would agree to be posted in Karamoja in those days and even today? They would rather be jobless and engage in some other vocation than risk their lives going to teach in Karamoja. Going to Karamoja in my days was like signing your own death warrant. But then again, there were people who gave up their lives just to help Karamoja. Those were missionaries. The nuns and the sisters at the convent knew exactly what they were up against on a daily basis, but they stuck it through.

While at school, my best part of class time was storytelling. With my cheeky disposition, everyone looked up to my turn to tell stories because they found them pretty humorous. I just used to love those sessions and would really look forward to them. This was, of course, in P1 and P2. Is it any wonder that one of my biggest passions these days is motivational speaking? It must have started back then, and it must be in my blood.

Another favorite part at school was physical education (PE). Remember, I never used to have time to play outside of school, and so PE was heaven for me. I loved playing netball, as I have already shared. I would look forward to PE with so much enthusiasm as it would just free me.

Apart from the caning I received for lateness and other misdemeanors, life in that school was not necessarily rosy. In fact, later on, after Uncle saw firsthand the suffering I was going through at the hands of my foster mother, he decided to enroll me in the boarding section of the school. That solved quite a bit of the problems I had then, but there were others related to health.

I remember the unbearable suffering I went through those days under the scourge of scabies. It was an epidemic that affected very many a child as it was also contagious. There was no adequate treatment for it. A person infested with scabies would really suffer physical and emotional trauma, not to mention the jesting that you would receive from other kids. There was also the jigger scourge to contend with, seeing that not anyone in school wore shoes. Those two scourges really made life difficult for us.

The scabies, however, took the trophy of skin torment on me. It was just too bad. Yet even in that condition, I still had to do all the work at home. There was a time when it was so rampant on me, and all I could do was to pocket it at all times.

It was on one of those days, at the height of that suffering, that a certain teacher picked on me. The teacher told me to get to the front of the class and put out my hands, which were covered by the most horrible sight of scabies. It was a moment of shaming. The teacher did this on purpose.

To date, I wonder what was in it for him. I wonder what he was gaining by doing that. He was a person in authority over my life. He had been given the express authority to mold me, shape me, educate me, and hone my potential. But here he was, doing the exact opposite. Again, such moments can be very defining. Such moments have a bigger potential of leaving a massive scar on the soul of a child than scabies causing scars on the skin.

The reason as to why I still remember that episode is that it was totally humiliating. The other kids laughed at me, and it affected me. In turn, I became aggressive and started fighting. Whenever someone would abuse me, I would fight with them because my self-esteem had already been killed.

* * *

One day, while at school as a boarding pupil, my life was just about to be turned upside down. I had heard many stories about the Karamojong warriors and had even spotted some during our excursions in fetching firewood. At those moments, we could run and evade them. It was like a consistent cat-and-mouse game. The cat knew the mouse was there, and the mouse knew the cat was there. It was who played best the hide-and-seek game that survived.

However, on that fateful day, there was no hiding to the seeking that the Karamojong raiders were doing. They decided that time around to invade the school. It was early in the morning, at around 6:00 a.m., that we looked up and saw in the school playground something that totally horrified all of us.

A few moments earlier, our early morning routines were rudely interrupted by the familiar and horrifying sounds of gunshots, only this time the blasts were closer to home—the shopping center just near the school. We were in the dormitory at that time. Of course, when you hear a loud bang, everything around you comes to a standstill. There is this fear that grips you and literally owns you. Your heart starts pounding at such a fast rate as blood flows through your body. At that moment, the word *priorities* gets its real meaning. That is when you know what the most important thing in your life is.

As the events were unfolding, the school administration swung into action and decided to lock us in the dormitories. However, when we shortly realized that the raid was not in the town center but that the school was the immediate and primary target of the raid, all hell broke loose. When the administration saw the school field full of warriors, they opened the dormitories, and the kids ran in different directions to the bush. I joined in the melee and took off, not knowing where I was going. I could not run home because I had to go through the school compound where the raiders were. I followed other kids and grown-ups as we ran for our dear lives. Our flight took us all the way to Natemeri in Northern Kenya! Everybody was on their own; your life first! I did not see Uncle or my foster mother.

Kenya was not such a strange place anyway. We had been there several times as we crossed the border to go buy basic needs such as soap, salt, and sugar. We could do this nearly every two weeks. In fact, in Amudat, you could use either Ugandan currency or Kenyan currency. The border was that porous. All along we thought we were doing the right thing until, later on, I came to understand that we were smuggling, something that was forbidden by the government of the day. In fact, in other regions bordering Kenya in the eastern region, when smugglers were caught, they would be punished by the antismuggling unit specially set up to rid the country of the vice.

At that time, the country was under the rule of Yoweri Kaguta Museveni, and its economy was recovering from the insurgency. In Karamoja, there was a shortage of basic things that we needed for day-to-day life, like sugar. From our location in the east, Kenya was approximately nineteen kilometers away. And that was the distance we covered that day, unplanned. And we covered that distance running for our dear lives and not walking to go buy a commodity!

The warriors entered the convent and ransacked it, taking nearly everything that they found in the stores. They raided the school specifically to steal and rob the food supplies. The school was well stocked with food at all times, being supplied by the church that oversaw the convent. By the time the raid was over, one kid had been butchered. She was the daughter of the local chief. And once again, I escaped that deadly raid with my life and lived to tell the tale.

We were told that the raiders had been given specific orders by their spiritual leader not to harm anyone at the school. Their task was to get into the school and get out of it with food. It turns out that the warrior who shot the kid dead was identified and also executed by the raiders themselves.

On our part, we stayed in Kenya as refugees for a day or so. I was together with people I did not even know, some group who came from the community who ran away from the warriors. My uncle looked for me. Everyone had run to a different direction. There were many other times that the raiders came, but this raid at the school was unlike any other. They raided around the center where we stayed. It was a life of fear, survival, and insecurity all throughout.

That was approximately the third time that I had a close shave with death or misfortune and survived to tell the tale. Have you ever seen a beautiful plant budding through the cracks of concrete? That is the total representation of my life, against all odds.

Part 2

Matters in My Own Hands

Chapter 6

The Pain of a Destitute Mother

Seven years can seem quite a lot, especially for young people. But it is so fleeting, and before you know it, you are no longer a toddler; you are now a teenager. Looking at the mundane existence that I had those days, I tend to wonder why people are allowed to live. Toward what end do we exist? Can you look at the life I was leading in those days? Wake up. Clean the house. Prepare breakfast. Bathe the kids. Go to school. Come back home to prepare and eat lunch. Go back to school. Come back home. Wash, cook, clean, repeat.

What is the essence of that life? What kind of hope does it represent? I am not so sure if I knew what the term *hope* meant or if it even existed. I do not know if I looked forward to the future. But I can tell you this: day by day, I had a determination in my spirit to never give up. My gifts and talents both of mind and body kept me going. That, I perceive, is one of the most obvious ways to know that God has set you apart for something.

If you are special and talented in any way, God has already marked you and even equipped you for a reason and for a purpose. Unfortunately, very many people take their talents and gifts for granted. Also, we have a way of life that negates the innate gifts and talents and emphasizes other things, such as school tests and examinations. These have their place, but they should not be at the expense of natural gifts and talents. The good news is that we are all gifted and talented in special and unique ways. So to me, gifts and talents are the first indication that God has a purpose and a plan for you.

43

The second thing that God has given us that makes us move on is dreams and aspirations. We are the only species on earth that can look forward to a better future and a better life. We are the only ones who can dream and plan and exert ourselves to see those dreams and plans come to fruition. So I may as well say that God speaks to us about our future through our dreams and aspirations. He then equips us with the gifts and the necessary talents to use to see these aspirations come to fruition.

Those two things are extremely important, for you can remove any and all physical resources that are needed to succeed, but if you still have dreams and aspirations, gifts, and talents, those two are enough to create a determination that will go far and wide to create the environment under which our hopes will be realized. I never knew all these things as a child growing up in Karamoja. But as I look back at my life with the benefit of hindsight, indeed I can see that the odds were never going to kill my assignment on earth.

Through a series of destitutions in a suffering region of Uganda, I finished my primary education in 1991 and sat for my final examinations. That was a milestone that only I was able to accomplish in our entire immediate family born of my mom and dad. Finishing primary education is always a rite of passage of sorts for very many people across the earth. You are no longer the same, and you are treated more like an adult. And then of course, there is that season of life that many a young person in Uganda long for: vacation.

Speaking of rites of passage, you need to understand that culturally, rites of passage in Uganda are taken very seriously. For example, for the Bagisu people of Eastern Uganda, male circumcision is a cultural must. For the Pokot people, however, female genital mutilation (FGM) is wildly practiced. In fact, the practice is so ingrained in the culture to the level that a real woman will be identified by having gone through that bizarre practice.

The culture is so unquestioned to the level that the women themselves volunteer to go through that. If you are not circumcised as a woman, you do not belong. You feel left out. You are not respected. So naturally, you will seek to go through the process in order to be part of the community.

Like I said earlier, if you had taken a look at me in those days, you would have never known that I was an Itesot from Katakwi. You would be mistaken to think that I was a native of Karamoja, born and bred there. I spoke the language; I basically fitted into the culture like a glove in a hand. It was not easy to distinguish between me and a native.

Therefore, it was only natural that as I grew up, I started craving to go through that rite of passage! One day, during the season of circumcision, my schoolmates and I hatched a plot to go out there and get "cut." Like I said, this was a hotly sought-after ceremony by many a girl. Much as the schools discouraged the girls from it, their bond to the culture and community was stronger than education. Girls would disappear from school for two to three weeks and reappear later as "women."

We were not just about to be left behind. We got together and psyched one another up and headed straight to the site. Uncle Nicholas was totally oblivious of this, and I am sure he will just be as surprised as you are when you are reading this. There are things we do in secret from our parents that only eternity will tell. The site where the rite of passage was being conducted consisted of two grass-thatched huts. In one hut, the actual cutting was being done. The other hut was where the girls who had been cut would be taken for healing.

When the five of us got there, of course, we knew what to expect. However, thinking what you know in theory is not the same as actually having experiencing it. The sight was a total horrible mess! I cannot begin to explain to you the extent of pain, cries, blood flow, and agony that I saw that day. A thin sweat broke on my brow, and my heart gathered pace, racing like a Ferrari. Friends, FGM is not something you can wish even for an enemy. It is a horrible practice, does not have any value, and totally mutilates a woman.

Besides, there are very many deathly stories that are told from this practice. Some women die. Others experience complications for the rest of their lives. I will never forget a schoolmate of ours called Halima. She was one of the most promising pupils in primary school for she had quick wit and a sharp brain. One day, during the circumcision season, she went and got herself cut. After a few weeks, Halima was back to school, and life proceeded as normal. A few months later on, however, Halima dropped out of school for she was pregnant. During childbirth, however, Halima developed complications and literally bled to death, a side effect of the genital mutilation.

While the horror was still playing on like some unreal thing before me, I developed such a gripping fear and was strongly startled and traumatized. Now some motivational speakers normally say that *fear* is "false evidence appearing real," but oh boy, aren't they wrong. That was not false evidence by any shot. That was not unreal. That was real! Other motivational speakers say *fear* stands for either "face everything and rise" or "face everything and run." The latter part of that statement was the best meaning of *fear* I ever had at that time.

Suddenly, I realized that my gift and talent for running was not just for a show and for competitions; it was also for flight. Ladies and gentlemen, I know for a fact that there are great feats that we achieve "in the dark," when no one else but God takes note. That day was my day. I do not think I have ever taken off like I did that day. I literally ran for my life, and chances are that I might have half ran and half flown! I posted my personal best!

There was no way in my life that I could allow myself to willingly go through mutilation in the name of a rite of passage. Besides, I wasn't even born in Amudat! I was born in Teso, and we do not do such things where I come from. Those were my strong excuses as I escaped with my life. That day, I escaped like a bird from the horror of FGM, and I lived to tell the tale. Three of my friends, however, were brave enough to go through with the procedure. They came from the region, and they were Pokot girls.

* * *

Uncle Nicholas organized a journey to go back to Katakwi in order to attend the last funeral rites of my late grandpa. We had never made it for his burial because of lack of finances and the danger in the transport in those days. I had not seen my people for years, and of course, this was exciting for me. As I have already mentioned, traveling to, from, and through Karamoja was a deadly affair in those days, but this time around, I was determined to go see my family.

I was so pleased to see my mom, and I know she was so happy and blessed to see me once again. To add to the pleasure of meeting for the first time in years was the news that I had completed my primary education. Mama was proud of me.

However, a very bitter war erupted between Mom and Uncle Nicholas. Mom discovered multiple wounds and scars on my body. It was obvious that these had been inflicted by beatings. I cannot begin to imagine the pain that my mom must have felt. If you are a parent and your children get to the point where they are suffering and you cannot help them, it tears you into pieces. It is more than psychological torture. You are helpless because probably there is nothing you can do to reverse the clock.

Seeing a single scar inflicted by a beating on your flesh and blood automatically transports you to that imaginary episode where your loved one is being inflicted by pain and misery. You can imagine the viciousness of the offender. You can imagine the howling of your loved one and their cry for help—help that never comes. And then you can imagine that this happens over and over and over again. There are parents who discover later on that their daughter was abused. Such loving parents, without counseling, can easily commit murder.

I cannot begin to comprehend the tumultuous emotions that the parents of those that have been abducted or kidnapped go through. It is far beyond human emotional pain to imagine a loved one in the hands of an oppressor, helpless. It must have messed up Mama's emotions so much. Probably the only mitigating fact was that I was nimble, alive, and happy. Probably she saw how industrious I was, and she was happy that I was turning into a responsible young woman. For some reason, I had not been subdued. God must have given me an incredible spirit of endurance. If children today will go through half of what I went through, chances are that they will be absolutely broken in soul, in spirit, and in body. But Mama was just one among the multitude of women out there who are helpless and cannot help their children.

I know for a fact that if it was up to her, she would never have allowed Uncle Nicholas to go back with me again. She would have held unto me forever and taken care of me. But Mama could not afford to take care of me. I was supposed to be going to the next level of my education. Taking care of the rest of my siblings was already a burden to my widowed mother. As much as she felt the physical pain of being separated from her child, there was nothing she could do to help me, even if she wanted.

I can see her imagining me in the hands of another woman, being mistreated, yet she was far away, unable to help. But I am glad that it was Uncle Nicholas that she was feuding with, for if it was his wife, a fellow woman, the story would have been so different. Uncle loved me, and so did his kids. In fact, they so loved me that they used to follow me up to class. But their mother was a different story altogether. She hated me and hated my mom too, although they had never met. She also hated the fact that Uncle loved me. Like I said, anytime they had their own feud in their marriage, I would be the recipient of the backlash. Yet I survived against this odd too.

I was to see my mother again later on when I was in senior 2. As already shared, traveling to Tesoland from Karamoja was not easy because of difficulty in transport and security and even economic upheavals. Traveling was a necessity, not a luxury. The situation continued all the way into the millennium. I know that once in a while, the raiders still do terrorize my people, but not with impunity as in the past.

Chapter 7

What's in Moses's Hands? What's in Betty's Eyes?

So after the vacation was over, I traveled back with Uncle Nicholas to Amudat. By the time we got there, the kids who were joining senior 1 had already reported to school. I was late for the first term. The prospect of me going back to school seemed so dim. Uncle Nicholas seemed not to have any plans for my further studies.

As a child, I had assumed that I would continue with my studies unhindered. Yet secondary school is not the same as primary school in terms of expenses for parents and guardians. There are some parents who will move heaven and earth to make sure that their children will get an education. We have been told over and over again that education is the key, and many people have taken it to heart. That is why you will find a destitute family that is just scraping by, doing all in their power to educate their children. This is done in the hopes that one day, every child will come back and wipe away their tears and their shame.

It is even more difficult for those in situations like mine. I know Uncle Nicholas was just scraping by too, and he had a family. Sending me to secondary school was nothing short of a long-term commitment, and I can understand why he was vacillating over this decision. I know that he loves me, and I know that if he had all the money that was needed, he would have provided for my school fees. Day in and out, I waited and waited to go to school, but nothing was materializing. For some God-ordained reason, I had become so attached to education and learning that I could not, for a minute, fathom a life without school. I had seen my mom left behind by her husband, who was a subparish chief struggling just to get coins to rub together. In fact, I know that she would go for months on end before seeing a single coin.

That realization made me want to study so hard that I would never have to be in her situation again. And that is the third determinant for success, I must add. I have already shared about talents and gifts. Then I shared about desires and aspirations. However, without hunger and determination, without having a powerful reason *why* you want something, it is possible to be overcome at the first huddle.

My biggest driving force was the need to complete my higher education so that I could lead a better life than what my dear mom lived. Second, I really desired to help my mother and siblings. It was such an insatiable hunger that I dare say, it might have been set there as internal fire by God himself.

So when I asked Uncle Nicholas about school, he kept telling me that he had no money! School was in session, and there was no indication that I would join. This was a very critical moment of transition for me that I believe if it never was handled well, I probably might not be where I am today. That small moment of changeover was critical, yet it could have easily been passed on and forgotten. *"There is no money"* is a statement probably spoken throughout the world every minute of every day, and if just left at that without a rebuttal, it can rob people of their entire destinies. That great teacher, the late Dr. Myles Munroe said that *"failure is nothing but the test of your resolve."* If you don't have your resolve tested, then your resolution will have no gravity.

In other words, when you promise to do something, life will test the promise. I had made a promise to myself and to life that I would never be caught in the abject poverty to the ilk that my mom was experiencing. I promised that I would study hard to rectify that situation. That resolve enabled me to learn English and Swahili all by myself while I was in primary school. But now, my promise and my resolve were being put on their first major test. All along, I had been coasting around life without a resolve, but when I became aware of what I wanted, I was self-motivated. That motivation had now hit a major brick wall for this teenage girl-child.

So what does a teenager who is hungry to go on with school, living in the most forgotten region of the country with an uncle who is unable to raise school fees for her do? What options does she have? Just two options: keep asking Uncle Nicholas and keep crying every day!

There are different types of crying that come out of teenagers. There are those who cry for clothes. There are those who cry because they have been mistreated or left out. There are those who cry just to get attention. There are those who cry because they do not want to go to school.

But I was not one of them. When all seemed lost for me, I cried for my future. I cried for my life. The cry for your life can be a dry, bitter, and painful cry especially when you do not see anything in the physical environment changing for the better. But cry I did day in and day out.

The cry of this magnitude bordered on grief, sorrow, despair, and desperation. Nothing could console me. Every day, when Uncle Nicholas thought the subject had been put to bed, he would find me crying, or I would keep asking him as if I never heard him the first time telling me that "there was no money."

I wanted him to understand me. I wanted him to feel my longing and hunger for an education. It meant the whole world to me to have a chance to go to secondary school. That situation continued until it was no longer a family affair. The neighbors heard my cries and saw my desperation on a daily basis. I had a neighbor called Stella. When her dad saw me in that state, he really sympathized with me and said, "If I had money, I would pay for this child to go to school." Of course, the neighbors added voice to my cries and started pleading with Uncle Nicholas to find a way for me.

Not only was Uncle Nicholas a father to many children; he was also disabled financially. After a season of sustained pressure from myself and the neighbors, Uncle Nicholas decided to take me to the remotest secondary school. The name of that school is Arengesiep. This literally means "the side that is red." This school had no fence and was easily accessible from all sides, and security was lacking. In fact, my primary school was much better than Arengesiep. At that school, you could not tell the difference between a child and a teacher. Big men and women were students there.

For all I know, some of them might have been the Karamojong warriors. You know, the wisest man who ever lived on this earth said, *"A person who is full of food will refuse honey. But to a hungry person, any bitter thing seems sweet."*[1] To me, that was much better than staying at home. If I had not pursued my studies, I would have preferred to be dead. So I welcomed the move to pursue my studies at that school. The school was located in an area called Nabilatuk in present-day Nakapiripirit District.

My dream was always to go to Kangole Girls, which was one of the best secondary schools in that region at that time. Uncle could not afford to take me there. In fact, he could not even afford to pay the full fees for me to study at Arengesiep. I remember, at that time, the school fees for first term was twenty-four thousand Ugandan shillings (seven dollars). Back then, it was quite an amount for a destitute person to manage to scrap around. In addition to the school fees, Uncle was also supposed to get me some necessities for school. This was the very first time that I got something to put on my feet: slippers.

My tears had worked magic, but I was not satisfied with the school at all. I did not like it, and I wanted to have a better chance elsewhere. However, this was heaven as compared to sitting at home without an education. At times, you aim for the stars and reach the clouds. By the time I was getting to my "clouds," however, it was only three weeks to the end of the term.

---

[1]   Proverbs 27:7

Uncle paid half of the school fees and left me at that school with absolutely nothing! *Pocket money* was a foreign terminology that my circumstances found exotic.

Again, another divine providence came in by virtue of my natural gifts and talents. I found that it was the athletics season at that school, and I promptly immersed myself in it. I came out the best in every category that I participated in. They found out that I was the best in all the short races as well as the long ones. I participated in one hundred meters, two hundred meters, and four hundred meters and won all those races! I also competed in high jump and long jump, where I emerged the best. So I was naturally selected to go and represent Arengesiep at the district competition. This was not new territory, unlike how it was at the primary school competition. I had already participated in athletics competitions and won. I can still remember the material day at the secondary school games.

This time around, I was fully aware of my gifts and talent in athletics, and I knew that I was up to prove it once again. The excitement in my bones made me feel nimble and restless, waiting for the one hundred meters to be flagged off. And by the time the command *go* was given, like a bird swift in flight, I flew off that ground barefoot and left dust, literally, behind all my competitors. There was no struggle, and there was absolutely no question about who would take the day.

In fact, that day, my triumph excited the school's games teacher so much that he earned himself a beating from the organizers of the competition. It turns out that I gave my challengers such a huge range to catch me, and by the time I crossed the finish line, the games teacher could not contain his excitement. He came and carried me shoulder high, showing how proud he was. I was so petite and little in those days. That was totally out of protocol.

In athletics, there are people who are allocated to receive numbers 1, 2, and 3 and be registered accordingly. The games teacher came from nowhere, oblivious of such rules, and took me away. Of course, the organizers caught up with him, probably not knowing who he was, and briefly gave him a beating and a stern admonition.

Now, there comes a time in life when a single event can alter the looks of something otherwise forgotten forever. Arengesiep was the remotest, most primitive school in the whole district. But when Betty entered the stage to represent that school at the district level, by the time the competitions were over, that school was on the map!

This too was the benefit of those endless tears that I cried, seeking to go to school. Chances are that if I relented and never pestered Uncle, this feat would never have been achieved. It was the first time in the history of Arengesiep that they won in anything. Their champion, however, was the most unlikely of all—that girl who wore a single dress for years and was now a proud owner of a new pair of slippers.

After that brief history-making feat, it was already time to go back home. School holidays were now at hand. So I had to travel back. The journey was divided into two legs. First of all, we were to take a car from Nabilatuk, where the school was located, to take us to Namaalu. From Namaalu, we would take another car that would now take us to Amudat. There was a small problem, however: Uncle had not left me with any cash, even that which I would use for transport back home! This was notwithstanding the horrible road network in the region, coupled with insecurity.

I, together with other students, resorted to ask for free rides from trailers that were plying that route. Fortunately for me, there was a trailer transporting ammunition. It had soldiers in it. We flagged it down, and thank God, it stopped. They ferried us all the way to Namaalu. It was not every day you get to be transported in an army trailer ferrying ammunition!

While at Namaalu, we were back to square one again, although nearer home. You need to understand that in those days, we did not have cell phones. Even the traditional analogue telephones were not available in the

Karamoja region. I would have called Uncle Nicholas, and he would have found out a way for me. However, at that point in time, I had to fend for myself. At Namaalu, however, there was a mission tractor, thank God! The mission tractors would move from one mission to another. The mission used tractors mainly because of the horrible road network that we had back then. So it turns out that at the exact moment that I needed help, a mission tractor was on hand in Namaalu!

We gleefully took the ride back to Amudat! Mission impossible? Hardly! I was happy to have overcome that small uncertainty on my own, and for the very first time, I was traveling under no care of my uncle! I looked forward to seeing him and his family back at home. Of course, there was that small matter of the pending school-fee balance and the fees for the new term. I had made it this far, and chances are that I would still make it! I was determined. However, when I got home, I do not think I was prepared for what awaited me there.

Chapter 8

An Unconnected Connection

The year 1981 would always be etched in the records of a certain girl from Tororo called Susan Anyango. She had been raised in a polygamous family having a total of fifteen children. Her father was, prior to his marriage, a man highly devoted to spiritual matters of the church and could easily have been a priest. However, when he married a second wife, priorities shifted. Her family was somehow cut short from his responsibility of taking care of them. Her poor mother was left alone to fend for the whole family.

She was the second last born on her mother's side, a family of six children, with four girls and two boys. Susan still remembered the big and benevolent heart of her mother. Susan's mom extended her heart of compassion to very many people in the community, especially to the poor people. They were so close to her. At first, this really bothered Susan. For example, a poor woman would come to their home and borrow her mom's nice Sunday dress in order to go for a visit. When this woman returned the dress, Susan's mom would ask her to keep it! This baffled Susan so much initially. At times, the dress would be returned unwashed, and Susan would pick up a quarrel with her mother over it.

But her mom would not change. What she was doing was not a mechanical thing; it came from deep down her sanctified soul. She would not struggle in being compassionate to the less fortunate in society. Soon enough, that compassion started inspiring the young girl Susan. She started noticing the poor in society and wanted to be able to do something about them. From as early as Susan could remember, she started feeling the call of God upon her life, and she was aware of it. Over the course of the years in her life, that call kept growing as she would observe sisters in the local convent. The trigger of it all, however, was the actions that her mom did on a daily basis—taking care of the less fortunate in society.

Susan's mom was a trained primary school teacher, and her dad was an inspector with the Ministry of Education. The two of them agreed that Susan's mom should stay at home and take care of the children. Of course, that was before there was a misunderstanding between them upon him marrying a second wife. Being an educator, Susan's mom understood the value of giving the girl-child an education. That was why she spared no cost or energy in taking all her six children through school.

Given that she could no longer go back to teach, she made ends meet by teaching other women in the community certain aspects of hygiene, cooking, and other things. Apart from that, she taught Susan and the family how to brew the alcohol locally known as malwa that would be sold in pubs around Tororo. During that time, drinking was not allowed at home. So the brewers would make deals with the local pubs to supply it. Susan's mother's malwa was popular because it was as thick as it could get, and with malwa, the thicker it was, the better. Her beer would never stay overnight for even one day, for people all over the community knew about its quality.

That was how she struggled and managed to give her children an education. The struggle continued as long as that was the only viable way of raising cash for school fees, up until Susan's brother-in-law, Mr. John Kidimu, came to the rescue later on. He had such a giving heart, and this would not be the last time we read of him.

To date, Susan looks back at the moment that John stepped up to take care of her schooling with so much gratitude. Indeed, we have no idea if this story unfolding right here would have been possible were it not for that little and seemingly unrelated action of John. Your action of kindness today for someone in life has the potential of reverberating over generations, unbeknownst to you.

Susan attended Namirembe Mixed Day and Boarding Primary School–Budaka for her primary education. She was one of the most intelligent pupils at her school. During that time in the seventies, passing the primary school leaving examinations was a big thing. From there, she went directly to a teacher's training college in Bukedea, Eastern Uganda, because it was free. Given the economic situation of her family, Susan could not proceed to the advanced-level school that she had been invited to. Teachers' college was the next obvious step because it had less economic pressure on her mother and family.

In fact, soon after she started teaching, she was the one who paid school fees for her sister, who was taking a course in nursing. In 1979, the year after a certain Betty Ogiel was born, Susan qualified as a trained teacher from Bukedea Teacher Training College. Because she passed pretty well, she was retained at the institution to teach and to serve as an example to others. This was for a period of two years. While there, her ambition to become religious intensified in her. Her inspiration came from the Franciscan sisters from Ireland. She really desired to be part of them; however, they were not taking Africans who aspired to become nuns under their tutelage. They nevertheless pointed Susan to the Society of the Sacred Heart Sisters, who were open to taking African girls who were interested in becoming nuns.

Soon after, she was posted by the government to Moroto District to teach. All along, the inspiration that she had seen in her mother as well as what she had observed from other people in church circles was growing in her more and more. She wanted to become a person who was religious. When she saw nuns, she would deeply feel a sense of being like one of them. The call upon her life, as it were, was not something that happened at once; rather, it was something that was growing on her over a period of time. Unbeknownst to her, God was ordering her steps and charting her path to be a difference maker in the lives of many people, especially to the girl-child.

So in 1981, Susan decided that she had to accelerate her progress to become a nun. That is the stage called aspirant. She was soon a postulant after a period of one year in her progression to become a nun. After this step, her next step was the novitiate training, which took a period of two years. This involved leaving everything behind and going for an intensive training.

As you are being trained, they monitor you to see if you are ready to progress. Susan did this in the formation houses of the Society of Sacred Heart Sisters in Nkozi and Ggaba in Kampala. Soon after, Susan was a young professed, a stage that takes six to ten years before going to Rome to take the final vows to be fully professed. It was at this stage that Susan went back to Karamoja and started teaching at Kangole Girls Secondary School.

Susan loved sports so much, and she immediately started forming sports teams. Each of the teams she formed performed extremely well. They represented the school at district levels in Moroto. One day, while at the district sports meeting, Sister Susan caught a glimpse of a sportsperson that impressed her to the core. The only problem was that this sportsperson was not a boy, but it was a girl—yours truly.

According to Sister Susan, she was mesmerized by my stamina in running races. I ran nearly all the races and participated in nearly all the sports disciplines and won. The manner of my winning was grand in that those who came second after me were more than four meters behind! Anybody could see that I had the raw talent in athletics. I ran one hundred meters, two hundred meters, four by four hundred meters, and eight hundred meters and won them all! This was done without the help of any kind of formal training or coaching. It was pure talent. To me, that is the ticket that the Almighty God gave me to open the seemingly locked doors of my life.

Sister Susan was so impressed by me, and she made a mental note. Later on, in the evening, Sister Susan called me aside for a small talk. It was this small talk that would later on define the progress of my life. Sister Susan planted in me the idea of furthering my studies at Kangole Girls where she was teaching. She asked me to make sure that I seek admission there once I was through with my primary level. I had briefly mentioned to her my predicament, and she seemed caring enough to make the invitation. I went back home feeling on top of the world. Of course, Sister Susan did not have a clue if I would one day make it to her school. It was about two or so years before I would be eligible to go to an ordinary-level school.

Looking back in retrospect, I am amazed at how critical one casual talk by two primary school teachers about one of their pupils was in shaping my destiny. At times, we want to call something a miracle when we can directly attribute its occurrence to God. At times, we forget that the little, indirect, casual, and sometimes unconnected occurrences are the way the Master Chess Player positions his pieces of the chessboard of life for the greater good. Had those two teachers not recognized my gift, I would never have represented Kalas Girls Primary School. This appearance at the district-level competitions might have just been a competition to me, but God was behind the scenes, making careful moves for the betterment of this girl-child.

Chapter 9

Donkey Left Behind

As I walked down the dusty roads of Amudat on my way from my first three weeks at secondary school, there was a mixture of emotions that I was going through. I was proud that I had been able to achieve this feat single-handedly, traveling all the way from school without Uncle's supervision. The few weeks I had been at Arengesiep were very fruitful to me, to say the least. I looked back with a sense of pride and satisfaction, having elevated that school to sporting history in athletics. I thought I would recount my exploits to Uncle with lots of glee, and he would be proud of me—but I was wrong.

My world was just about to be hit by an unexpected bombshell that would send me reeling in shock and disbelief. A young teenager like me could not be able to handle the situation that I was just about to find out.

In those few twenty-one days, my whole life as I had known it since coming to Amudat was altered by a decision Uncle Nicholas made—to move out of Karamoja. He had asked the Kalas Primary School administration for a cross transfer back to Teso and was granted. I am not so sure if that had been in the offing all the while or if it just happened while I was in school.

Uncle separated with his wife and went back to his homeland. The thing is that he did not inform me that he would do this. But he had the presence of mind to know that I was in school and would be coming back for the holidays. So he left the keys to the house at the neighbors.

When I got into the house, every single thing was intact; it was as if he would be coming back shortly. However, Uncle never ever went back to Amudat, save for when he had to attend a burial two and a half decades later! At that young age, I was abandoned by my guardian. I was now officially on my own!

So what does a girl with only slippers for her feet with a pending school-fee balance and a huge dream to continue with her education do? Up to today, I do not remember grasping what the magnitude of being abandoned by the only person who loved me in Amudat meant for me. There were some options for me to look at even at that young age. I was not even a native of Karamoja. I did not have any other relative to take care of me. Moved from my ancestor's home to a distant and hazardous land, I was now left alone in that place, totally clueless of what to do.

Kids need guidance and mentoring especially as they go through the tricky transitions in their lives. Most especially, they need the protection and provision of their parents who are meant to be stewards of their lives till they graduate to be young adults. Even young adults will not make it in life without the constant benefit of having a reference point from an adult who has gone through life and seen it all, having experience and wisdom.

But there I was, tender and young, not even an adult, alone in Karamoja, abandoned. It was enough to be born destitute. It was enough to lose my father. It was enough to be separated from my mom. It was enough to be mistreated by my foster mom. It was enough to grapple with poverty. It was enough to barely make it to secondary school. Up until now, I had handled all those odds blow-by-blow, and I was at par with them. This latest blow though was unbelievable as it was unexpected!

I sat down in that empty house, and all manner of thoughts rushed through my young brain unfettered. "Why?" must have been the biggest question on my mind that day. This question was directed at life itself. Why me and why this? Why not leave me alone for a while? Why not give me a break?

I thought Uncle loved me. Why would he do this to me? Was I such a big burden to the only person whom I thought cared for me? My small brain knew of the existence of the Divine, but he was as silent as Uncle's absence, or so I thought. The state of sitting down, doing nothing can easily take a toll on someone, and before you know it, you may want to end your life, finding no meaning to live.

After a while of sitting there and pondering on life's biggest questions, I noticed that my zeal and hunger for education had not been quenched. I noticed that I had defied so many odds so far and was able to sneak into secondary school albeit for three weeks. This was an achievement that none of my siblings would have been able to boast of as at that time, especially those who were older than me. Quickly, my mind shifted from the pensive and reflective mood and started dreaming, aspiring, and thinking ahead. How I learned to do that, I do not know.

First of all, I knew that I could not risk my life to travel back to Teso. I was young, and I did not know the way back. Besides, I did not have any money to finance such a move. I also knew firsthand the kind of life that awaited me in Teso. It was a life that I knew I could not want to be part of. I was fully aware that if I ever decided to go back to Teso, the slim chances that I had for my education would totally disappear. I knew for a fact that my mother would not help me, even if she wanted to, because she did not have the capacity to. I am not in a position to remember the real emotions that I went through when I was abandoned. I might have been scared. I might have cried. I might have felt totally unwanted here on earth. But still, deep down my soul, there was something else that was still in operation.

The same reason that made me cry for school was still in play. I really had a very strong urge to forge on in my life. So I took stock of my situation. Looking around the house, I discovered that there was a good store of cereal maize. I immediately hatched a plan, and I knew exactly what I would do—I would brew malwa. Uncle's wife had taught me all there was to know about this trade, right from brewing to selling, and I knew I could pull it off.

I think that one thing that was a character trait that I developed is hard work. I used to work hard that I acquired a nickname, *Punda*. People would see me and would say among themselves, *"Huyu msichana anafanya kazi kama punda milia!"* (This girl works so hard like a donkey!) And so Punda became a name for which the whole community in Amudat identified me with. This definition was not complete, however, without a reference to the beatings that I would get from my stepmother. In fact, the name Punda predominantly implied that I was being mercilessly beaten up like a wild donkey.

As I tried to settle and find my bearings after being abandoned, I thought I had found pity in a certain neighbor's eyes. She must have noticed my dire situation and tried to show the littlest compassion she could muster. That neighbor would call me and give me food on an occasional basis. Today, as I look back, I realize how naive and innocent I was as a child. The only definition I can remember of this woman is that she was a wicked person, yet at that time, I exulted in the fact that she was trying to help me.

There was this day that she invited me to her house for supper. The meal was vegetables commonly known as *sukuma wiki*, accompanied by maize meal commonly known as *posho*. I devoured that meal with lots of gratitude. For some reason, she had prepared it so well, and it was such a sweet meal.

However, when I got back home, all hell broke loose. I had a very serious stomachache down in my intestines. The pain that I was feeling can easily be equated to the pains of childbirth. This was the very first time in my existence that I was going through this kind of illness. I was alone in the house, and I was scared. I could not get out and seek help. The whole night, I kept tossing and turning and crying and curling myself into a knot. I do not know how well to describe the pain that I went through that night.

Looking back, I am almost sure that what I ate that evening was poisoned. You know, at that young age, I had already had several brushes with death. First was when I was traveling with Uncle back to Teso for a funeral. We survived an ambush by a matter of a few minutes! God spared my life that way. The next was when the warriors invaded our school, slaying one kid. I escaped death by a whisker once again. This was another opportunity for me to brush my shoulders with death. For some reason, I survived. I do not remember going to seek medical attention anywhere, but in the morning, I prepared myself some black tea, took it, and felt better gradually. I do believe that it was God who spared my life from the jaws of death that day. And if I thought that this was the last time that I would have a brush with death, I was seriously mistaken.

I went back to this woman's house that day and recounted how my night was miserable as I battled with stomach pain. Even at that young age, I could see guilt written all over her face. From that moment on, I never trusted her again, and I never once got a meal from her. I was officially on my own, fending for myself. Probably that episode gave me more impetus to improve on my local brewing business.

My malwa was ready for consumption each morning. My customers, who included part of the warriors in the community, loved to brush their teeth with malwa. So by 6:30 a.m. every morning, I was in my spot selling malwa. By 8:00 a.m. thereabouts, I was back in the house to start the preparation process all over again. That became the cycle of my life.

And why would I be doing this? you might be asking. I can tell you that I never did expend the proceeds from my small business. I kept all the monies that I got, save for what I would use daily for food. I could have bought shoes and meat, things that I dearly needed, but I kept all that money. Of course, I bought myself some dresses to wear, which, to me, was a great feat. How many teenagers worked and bought dresses for themselves?

Ladies and gentlemen, I brewed malwa for my future. This was the second most intentional thing I ever did about my future. After knowing what I really wanted in life, I could say that the end justified the means. As a young girl three or four weeks back, all I could do to fulfill my dream for school was cry and seek pity. That intentional move bought me a chance at a remote and primitive school for which I had school-fee arrears.

However, the interim period of three weeks grew this young girl-child into a grown-up fighting for her life. You could have seen me brewing local drinks and labeled me a destroyer of families, or a wine bibber or an addict or spoiled. But you would be wrong. I did all that I knew I could with all that I had in my hand, and looking back, I am not so sure if I would be where I am today had I not brewed malwa and waragi. Well, obviously, if you look at it from the angle of the Divine, probably there could be a better way to go about it, but I did not know that better way! I brewed my future for I was facing insurmountable odds in life at that time.

One of the buzzwords in the business arena is the word *scale*. When you have an innovative idea and you are seeking for someone to fund it, they normally ask the question, can that idea scale? In other words, can it be sustained, and can it be expanded to cover not just your present customers but also those in other regions?

I was sharp enough in those days to note that the mom of a friend of mine was also a good brewer. As for her, she had a market niche in neighboring Kenya. When I heard about it, I determined to smuggle my brew across the border to Kenya. So I approached her and talked to her about it. You can see I learned several aspects of business at that young age. I learned how to negotiate business deals. I learned how to grow my consumer base. I learned how to be always on time.

I also learned how to take risks and "scale" the business in unchartered territories. You know, someone said, *"He who has a 'why' to live can bear almost any how."* The cost of getting to school for me was negligible as compared to the hunger of learning and getting a better life than what my dear mother was experiencing.

So when I talked to my friend's mom about joining her in a smuggling excursion to Kenya, I must have made a great impression, for she allowed me to accompany her. I went home and made sure that my brew was ready, set lock, stock, and barrel for the day of smuggling. Like I had mentioned earlier, smuggling was a weekly thing that we were engaged in Karamoja.

However, this was a new gig. We always went to Kenya to buy supplies and bring them back to Karamoja. This time around, I was exporting illicit brew illegally to that neighboring country. In effect, I was an enemy to two governments: the Ugandan government and the Kenyan government. But I was not doing this for fun. I had a pressing need that I had to fulfill—fund my secondary education.

On the material day of smuggling waragi to Kenya, we met and packed our stock carefully. We concealed it in gunnysacks full of clothes, and off we went. I must say that I was a bit apprehensive, but I dared cross the border with my contraband. The first time we did this, we were very successful. There was no incident that we encountered. Naturally, when such a feat is accomplished, you tend to throw caution on the wind, and you want to go back and ride your luck. So before long, we were at it again, crossing the border with our sacks of waragi, pretending that we were transporting clothes.

In those days, it was common knowledge that the Kenyan policemen were more ruthless than the Ugandan ones. One never really wanted to fall into the hands of the Kenyan police, especially being on the wrong side of the law. It was a scary thing. On the second trip in our excursion, we got bold enough to decide to sell our brew farther into the Kenyan territory than the previous time. It turned out that there was a pickup truck that was going to the direction we sought, so we boarded it alongside other people that we did not know. Of course, they were Kenyans. Midway through the journey, our waragi boldly announced itself by producing a very strong and distinct scent.

"Mama, what are you transporting in your luggage?" asked one man.

"Oh, these are clothes," my elder companion responded pleadingly. I knew right there and then that our goose was cooked. It turned out that the men in that truck were plain-clothed police officers, and they had caught us red-handed in the vice of smuggling.

There I was, a young girl who was abandoned by her uncle deep in Kenyan territory in the presence of Kenyan police officers who knew that I was transporting illicit brew! That day will still be etched in my mind for years to come. I could feel blood running away from my face. My looks betrayed me, and there was no way I could wipe that guilt of my face.

My heart pumped in my chest so hard I knew someone would hear it. I am so sure those police officers obviously saw the terror that was printed on my face. "How about this child?" pressed on the police officers. "My son, these are just clothes," offered pleadingly the woman I was smuggling waragi with, my accomplice in crime.

The situation was only saved by another police officer, who said, "Leave the old woman and her daughter alone. They are merely trying to eke out a living in these tumultuous times we live in."

And that is how we escaped with a whisker and escaped from being detained and prosecuted in Kenya for the vice of smuggling and being in possession of illicit brew. That was another close shave. Had we been arrested, I do not know what would have transpired.

Chapter 10

Bye-Bye, Amudat!

Soon enough, it would be second term at Arengesiep Secondary School. I went back and paid the balance of the fee that Uncle Nicholas was unable to pay, plus a deposit of the second-term school fees. My enterprise was profitable enough to take care of my school needs to such an extent that I paid all my second-term and third-term fees.

Meanwhile, I was allowed to stay in Uncle Nicholas's house by the primary school administration. I will never understand that benevolence. I do not know if it was because there was nobody to occupy the house or if they knew my predicament and they just wanted to help. Besides, I was brewing malwa in the school compound!

One day, however, I made a decision. After realizing that I had a bit of money, I took a bold step and sought admission to Kangole Girls, the school of my dreams. I approached a local priest and asked for transportation to that school on the day that they would be traveling in that direction, and he agreed.

At times, you have to take matters in your hands in order for your dreams to come to fruition. I think intention is a very strong asset and spiritual capital necessary for success. However, intention alone is not enough. You have to do something, anything, even if you think it is "just trying" in order to move closer to your goal.

In fact, trying is the only way you can get feedback concerning your dream. There were so many odds against me joining Kangole Girls. But I knew that

I deserved it. I knew that I was intelligent, and I knew deep down my heart that I did not belong to Arengesiep. Knowing is one thing, but refusing is another.

It is the same thing that happened when I refused to stay at home until Uncle Nicholas got me admission to secondary school. There are many people who know, and in fact, they keep telling themselves, "You know what, I am better than this." However, they do not do anything positive to change their situation. Some may have no way out whatsoever. But I have learned that life is like that old giant called Goliath.

Every morning, you wake up with dreams, and life's Goliath taunts you daily, trying to break your resolve. Life calls you names and makes you cower at its enormous size. That story, however, tells us that the battle is never for the swift and for the strong and for the mighty. The battle belongs to those who trust in their god and take a step forward to conquer their mountains.

Kangole Girls was a deep-seated desire for me even before I was through with my primary education.

When the day came, the priest took me to Kangole, and I had to negotiate with the head teacher of that school. When was the last time you saw a teenager asking for admission in a secondary school all by herself? Even at that young age, I knew a few things about life. I knew how to play the poker of life. I knew that God had blessed me with intellect fit enough for the ilk of Kangole. I also knew that God had blessed me with the natural gift and talent of sports and, in particular, athletics. I knew that a school like Kangole Girls would greatly benefit from me. I also knew that the school did not operate charities, and that was why I armed myself with the whole amount of the first-term school fees: proceeds from my local brew! I was prepared. I was hungry, and I was ready.

My dream had been simmering in a distance, but that very day, I was standing on it, staking my strong claims on it. Nothing could stop me. Parent or no parent, guardian or no guardian, I was at Kangole to claim my dream. Never mind the little fact that there was no advertisement for vacancies for senior 2 at Kangole. Vacancies are always made for senior 1 and never usually for other levels. But that did not stop me. I knew that I could not wait anymore.

I also knew that I did not deserve to be at Arengesiep. I somehow felt that Kangole was my destiny. It was J. F. Kennedy who once said in his famous Moon Speech that the future would not be built by those who sat and waited. It would be built by those who were proactive and took actions and risks. I took the risk of being rejected, but for me, it was better to be rejected after making my case than to sit at home and settle down in Arengesiep.

That is what I have seen very many people do. When those who are better built, better equipped, intelligent, and gifted come across pressure in their lives, they settle for less. They start saying, "A bird in the hand is worth two in the bush." Well, the bird in my hand was not a beautiful one. It was ugly. In fact, it was injured and about to die. I did not want it in my hand. It would be better for me to let it go and go to the bush and hunt for the bird that I really did desire. And that was exactly what I did.

When I got to Kangole Girls, I found that the head teacher in charge was a nun. I told her my story on how I was the best in athletics at the district level in Moroto. For some reason, I did not share my predicament of being abandoned and being without parents and my dad passing on and my mom being destitute! By divine providence, I only put my best foot forward, literally selling myself to that school by telling them how they would benefit from me. I was not looking for pity. I was looking for an opportunity.

How I learned to do that, I do not know. But that was the style I used. Of course, in sales, there is something we call objections, and for the sake of Kangole Girls, the objection was school fees. I knew I had made a great pitch, and not only did I sell the fact that I would represent the school; I also think that other salient issues of communication, confidence, and negotiating skills must have upped my pedigree to the head teacher. Of course, we expect the nun in her to also have some level of compassion for people who are in situations like mine.

However, I did not play to the compassion tune. I knew that it would not work. "So what about the school fees?" When that question came, I knew that I had gotten my admission. I had accumulated lots of cash in my brewing enterprise. That very day, a teenager, against all odds, got admission to the school of her dreams and fully paid for that admission on the same day all by herself! The rest, as they say, is history.

I went back home via a truck and bought myself a metallic suitcase for school. I also bought myself other supplies and proudly admitted myself to Kangole Girls School in Moroto District of Karamoja for the first term in senior 2 in 1993. Ladies and gentlemen, that was the last time I would see Amudat, a place that shaped me against all the odds of my life. I decided that I would not go back there again.

Chapter 11

Refusing Status Quo

Getting into Kangole Girls was a dream come true. I could not have been more proud of myself that day as I walked into the school compound. That was, to me, life by design right there. I knew what I wanted, went for it against all odds, and got it exactly how I wanted it. It may sound as if it is that straightforward, but the truth is that it is not.

One major thing I have learned is that the status quo is a very powerful force. The status quo, unlike how most people think, is not static. Status quo is an active force, always pulling you back and goading you to not pay the price for your dream's fruition. It must be countered by another internal force and drive. This internal drive must, of necessity, be greater than the status quo. And this is where very many people dump and drop their dreams, because of the push and pull between status quo and dream.

The truth of the matter is that no dream worth pursuing will come through waiting and wishful thinking. When you conceive a dream, the first opposition to it is your status quo. It will not stay silent and be unchallenged. It will fight back. The dream, on the other hand, is delivered not through a path of no resistance. In fact, dreams are delivered best when the road of total resistance is taken and conquered. But then again, we need to realize that conquering one frontier ushers us directly into another new status quo, which has to be conquered at some point if we are to grow.

I would realize this truth not so long after becoming a student of Kangole Girls Senior Secondary School. There was still so much to conquer, and I had just learned the initial steps. Indeed, as I write today, there are still so many things and so many frontiers that I am yet to conquer. What I do have, however, is the DNA of a conqueror that was acquired both through design and through life forcing its lessons on me.

Speaking of lessons, I really did enjoy the lessons at school, and as had been my tradition, I was a top performer. I think the head teacher must have been vindicated for giving me a chance. I did not want to let her down. Soon enough, we were sitting for our first-term exams, and we would be going home. The word *home* was about to take a different twist in my life.

As already shared, I had determined that I would not go back to Amudat. I wanted to go to my real home and meet my people. It was my heart's desire. However, this too had a challenge that I had to overcome. Remember, I was alone in Amudat and did not know our home back in Teso. I did not know how to get there alone. The last time I was there, I was accompanied by Uncle Nicholas. My resolve, however, was made. Yet at times, what people call luck and coincidence normally play a major part in our lives. I think nothing in life just happens arbitrarily. There is a reason and a purpose for everything under the sun. And I have learned that much as our lives are not that straightforward and the means and methods of getting what we want are not straightforward, I know that there is a chance for luck and coincidence shaping it.

In my situation at that time, luck was my looks. Kangole Girls, of course, admitted students from different parts of the region, including my homeland, Teso. Back in Tesoland, my own brother Samson was a catechist in the local Catholic church. He was stationed in Katakwi. As providence would have it, some of the girls at Kangole attended this church! So when they took one look at me, it reminded them of none other than my brother. They saw a very striking resemblance between the two of us. They kept looking at me and would not just bring themselves to let the matter rest. Finally, they approached me and asked, "Are you in any way related to Samson?" I was pleasantly surprised.

Answering them in the affirmative, I informed them that he was my blood brother. I informed them that I was not a Karamojong and that I was only raised in Karamoja but that I was actually an Itesot. I asked them if they knew where my brother was and if they could take me to him. They confirmed, and we set a date later on when we would take a break for the holidays. To me, that was an answer to my longing to be reunited with my family. I couldn't have asked for such a better timing.

Meanwhile, Uncle Nicholas never went back to Amudat for more than twenty-five years! To date, I do not know what he would have told my mom if she asked him of my whereabouts. The truth is that he did not know what was transpiring in my life. He would not have any information to share with her. Should anything have happened to me, he would not even have known.

The day that I had been looking forward to the whole term came. We were just about to start our holidays, and that was the day that I would bring to effect my decision of not having to go back to Amudat. I had never traveled a long distance alone or at least without the covering of an adult like Uncle Nicholas. That would be the day that, for the first time in my life, I would be spending a considerable amount of time with my family members.

The plan was already in place for us girls to link up with my brother in Katakwi. This was the easy part since the girls who came from Katakwi knew their way around. Of course, the transport system was as pathetic as pathetic could be. The most common form of transport was through lorries. Kangole Girls stepped in beautifully. Our school owned a lorry that was used as a multipurpose vehicle. It could transport food, construction equipment, water, as well as students to and from functions. Buses, taxis, and cars were an exotic thing back then. Besides, they would not venture our region because of the twin problems that our region posed: poor road network and massive state of insecurity.

However, for us, our school lorry was heaven. We even had a name for it. We called it Pajero! In those days, it was the dream of a pupil or a student to take a ride in the Pajero to go represent the school in sports or choir or any other thing that the school was involved in. I remember using the Pajero on several occasions to go represent the school in athletics.

On one such occasion, the athletics meeting was taking place in Western Uganda, specifically at Fort Portal. That was the very first time that I passed through Kampala City. Unfortunately, it was at night, but I was very mesmerized. Now, traveling in the Pajero needed special arrangements. You would not just get in and sit down. Actually, for the most part, we would be lined up against the "walls" of the Pajero with our backs against it. Then, we would have our hands up touching the rails of the walls of the Pajero.

Picture someone on the cross, but at least with their hands not spread horizontally but lifted just above their heads. That was the position we were required to travel in, regardless of how long the distance was. In fact, this was the norm not only in Uganda but in very many African schools at that time. You might think that this was torture for us, but you would be wrong. Traveling in a Pajero going just about anywhere was pure bliss. We looked forward to this with as much enthusiasm as we would when going for a trip to a location that we loved.

So Kangole Girls provided the Pajero to drop the students around the district, but only at the major shopping centers. So we were dropped at Katakwi that day, and the girl who knew my brother's place directed me hand in hand right to his doorstep. Apart from being a catechist, he had a small kiosk or stall where he sold small things like sweets, biscuits, and matchboxes.

My reunion with my brother was quite unceremonious. However, when I saw his shop, my heart was happy for I knew then and there that there would be no problem settling my school fees! I knew that finally I was in the presence of family who cared and that the struggle I had had with my school fees was a thing of the past.

You know, for us kids, we did not know so much about the economics of the moment. Back in the day, anybody who had a shop was considered well-to-do, regardless of what they actually did sell in the shop. My brother's wasn't a shop, so to speak; it was a small stall. Another interesting thing came to note; Uncle Nicholas was actually living and teaching at a school in that area!

I knew that I would no longer work for my school fees. There are those moments in life when this saying gets life and meaning: *"You never really know how strong you are until being strong is the only possible thing for you."* Up to that point, taking responsibility of my own life was the only option I had to be strong. And as I did that, it was ingrained in my psyche to such an extent that it became normal.

So right there in Katakwi, for the very first time in years, I came to the stark realization of what a burden of my own life I had been carrying. I could have as well just heaved a sigh of relief after being reconnected with my blood brother and my very own Uncle Nicholas. It was a happy day for me. It was a very big milestone. I knew that I had been vindicated in my decision not to go back to Amudat. I must have felt proud of myself as I settled down in Katakwi over the school holidays. The combination of Uncle Nicholas and my brother surely sorted me out once and for all; no longer would I have had to work to pay my own school fees.

During the holidays, I would oscillate between my brother's house and Uncle Nicholas's place. The subject of my school fees was never brought up; neither did I have any doubt or worry about it.

Part 3

My Real Enemy: Poverty

Chapter 12

Spirit and Knowledge

The end of holidays came. I was ready to head back to my very own Kangole Girls. That school was like my own baby. You know, if you are a mother, you know the pains of childbirth, and for some reason, you get so attached to your children that even when they grow and have their own families, they will still be your babies. Kangole Girls was my treasure. My heart was fully there, to add to the fact that I really did cherish the idea of studying.

However, I realized that nobody was catering to me. The subject of my going back to school was not raised either by my brother or by Uncle Nicholas. Effectively, I was back to ground zero! I could not believe that I was at this predicament again. For a minute, I must have regretted closing my local brew business. My brother thought that Uncle Nicholas would sort out my school fees. In his reasoning, Uncle had been given the responsibility of taking care of the family. Officially, he was the one in charge. He said, "Uncle Nicholas took you and promised to educate you. You should go to him to fulfill his responsibilities. As for me, I cannot educate you because I do not have the resources to do so."

This broke my heart so much. My assumption was that my school fees would be paid without a hitch. At least I had done the difficult part of securing a position at Kangole Girls, or so I thought.

Uncle Nicholas, on his part, retorted, saying that my brother should be well able to take up the responsibility. After all, I am his flesh and blood sister. Uncle said that when I get married and the family paid bride price, my brother would be one of the chief beneficiaries. He intimated that he too was far too stretched to include me in the economy of his family. Looking back, I really do understand him.

You see, taking a child to secondary school is no mean feat. In fact, in communities that are hard-hit by poverty, schooling is never a priority, especially for the girls. The most plausible option for girls is usually to have them married off. That is exactly what the case was with my dear mother. She never did go to school because it was never a priority.

You know, you can measure the progress of a community by looking at the succeeding generations. If the same trouble that the previous generation faced is still the same predicament that the current generation is facing, then we are having a big problem in that society. The hold of poverty in my clan and family was not quite broken. Years after my mom had been married off, there I was, facing the very same reality.

There was a difference though. I was not a willing party to it. As much as nothing was said about it, I knew deep down in my heart that I must go to school and that there was no other option for me. It was a non-negotiable matter, already settled! The details would have to take care of themselves. That non-negotiability is what has shaped my life for the better.

Much as poverty had its tight hook on us, I was not just about to roll over and let it deliver one more blow on another member of the clan. I wanted to go back to Kangole, but I was stuck. I had no options. That, of course, brought the memories of my predicament in Amudat, just a few months prior to that. It seemed to me like the interval between my setbacks was very short. The greatest paradox, however, is that a small teenage girl was able to mobilize resources on her own and pay her school fees in full for three terms at two different schools, but two adults could not replicate that feat.

I heard a preacher one day lamenting that at times, a single mother can take care of seven children and even send some of them to school, yet when they all grow up, they can't even take care of their mother! Such situations exist in our world. I think it comes down to heart energy and priorities. My brother and uncle did not have the same heart energy that I had with my education. My heart was in my education more than a full percentage. Uncle and my brother had other priorities. As much as they loved me and were proud of me, they did not have enough heart energy to move my mountain. It was exactly two years since I unleashed the weapon of crying to move the mountain of lack of school fees. That weapon was potent enough to land me at Arengesiep, three weeks before the close of the school term.

Honestly, I did not have any new innovation on that weapon. I had not invented another method that would help me get unstuck. So it was all that I could do on a day-to-day basis—cry. This was a daily thing for me as I sought to get out of the predicament that I faced. I must have worn my brother down with my crying. I was home for three full weeks as school sessions went on. But I made up my mind that I had to go back to Kangole, my beloved school.

I told my brother that if he only got me bus fare, that would help me. I was walking in faith, not knowing what awaited me every single day. Finally, my brother was able to put some resources together and got me the exact amount of money that I needed for my transportation. There was no addition to that money, not even the equivalent of the same to come back should I be rejected at school.

As a young teenager, I was living by faith, not even knowing what it was. And that is how multiple millions live each day across the world. There are some people who do not have a clue where their next meal will come from. That situation is repeated daily for years on end. At the end of the day, all they think about is a meal. Thinking of something else is pure luxury. In fact, such kind of thinking is treated as dreams that will never materialize. I tell you, poverty is a bad and powerful foe. It has imprisoned so many people. If you can get people to stop thinking and just move on survival mode, such people cannot see progress come in their lives.

The case was different with me. For some reason, I had the fortitude, courage, and determination to think of a better life. I knew that the only way I could see my dreams come to fruition would be through getting a quality education. So I gratefully took that money after wiping away my tears, prepared my few belongings on earth, and set on a journey that I knew not where it would take me.

It was purely like Father Abraham. I have no idea what went through my mind as I traveled back to Kangole. My life was not in my own hands anymore. My life was placed squarely in the hands of the head teacher at Kangole and the school administration. In my heart, I had the confidence that I would find mercy in her sight.

That is another interesting thing about mercy. Mercy is not like rain that pours down on the just and the unjust. Mercy and grace are given to those who seek it. It is available for all, yes, but not all get it. Some people give up on the way. Such people will find it very difficult to access the mercy that they do need.

In fact, at some points in our lives, the only thing available to us to usher us to the next level is grace and mercy. That, however, does not mean that we sit in our stuck situation waiting for the mercy to come looking for us. We need to build the road to mercy by hope and determination.

Placing your life in someone's hands is a literal thing that is done by taking the step and doing all that is in your power to get to them. That was what I was doing as I carried all that I owned on earth in a metallic box and headed to Kangole Girls. I had no idea where the school fees would come from, but I knew that I had to study. I knew that I needed the opportunity. The hardship in the travel through the punishing road terrain was no hardship. It was nothing compared to what I faced, trying to secure another term in school without any money down.

As I got to the school compound and on to the office of the administrator, I knew I had to face the brutal facts of my life. All I did was to promise the school administration that the money would be paid. As I reassured them, I also knew that I had no clue of how it would be done. Amid that predicament, I kept studying. I kept feeding my hunger for learning.

School administrators the world over who are compassionate enough to allow kids even two weeks in school without fully paying their school fees should be lauded again and again. I know, of course, that schools have bills to settle. I know that some schools are pure business entities. Whether that is the case or not, every school incurs expenses in their bid to educate the next generation. These expenses can only be recouped through payment of school fees. I know some schools have stretched themselves to the limit just to give a child or two a chance. I know of others that have bursary schemes that help multiplied thousands around the world to get an education. I know that there are some governments that are championing free primary and secondary education where the expenses on parents are reduced to affordable levels.

Even so, there are still hundreds of thousands of destitute parents and guardians who do not have sufficient means to send their children to school. I also understand that the United Nations has declared education to be a human basic right. All these laudable moves, however, do not negate the fact that there are expenses incurred in education and that someone has to settle them. I cannot begin to imagine how many people out there have missed chances of getting an education just because they did not have the necessary finances. Such people have very many odds for success in life.

The world looks down, by default, on people who are not educated. These days, a degree holder has more advantages than a diploma holder, at least at face value. That is the way our current world operates. At such a young age, I knew that it was true that education was the key. If I had to live a better life than the one my destitute mother led, I had to scrape by until I got an education.

Finally, there came a time that the school administration sent me back home for nonpayment of school fees. That was the very first experience in my life, but it was nothing new—I was already used to disappointments. By that time, one would be excused to think that I could easily give up. The pain of getting an education was proving to be just too much for me! But God had given me a very intelligent mind, fortitude, and determination. I knew that I was suited for school and that I had the brains for it. I was passing my exams, and I was not struggling so much. Honestly, if I had struggles with my studies, chances are that I could have easily thrown in the towel and called it quits. But I didn't.

In the world today, there are very many talented people that give up just because there is seemingly no door immediately open to them. My advice is that we need to keep asking where the doors are. We need to keep seeking for where the doors are. And then we need to keep on knocking on the doors once we find them. The truth of the matter is that the doors are always there. It is just that they are not obvious. If we ask long enough, seek ravenously enough, and knock hard enough, a way can always be found.

However, all these are tied to understanding the real reason behind our asking, seeking, and knocking. For me, I determined that I would not be a victim of abject poverty like my dear mother was. I hated poverty with a passion, yet it was beside me like a close friend. It was around me, and I could not deny it. Nevertheless, I fought whatever dregs of poverty were seeking to imprison me especially in my mind. I knew that it was just a matter of time for me to overcome it, and so far, I had shown it what I was made of. But poverty kept fighting back.

In all my life, I have never seen such a relentless and well-equipped force as poverty. It never gives up. It keeps stalking and slaying its victims shamelessly day in and out. But poverty is a liar in the true sense of the word. It lies that once you have it, there is no way out. It lies that you cannot get out of it or outsmart it. It lies that it is such a monstrous big giant that cannot be overcome.

Poverty is a liar. It revels in the misery of people, making humans who are supposed to be princes and princesses be reduced to scavengers on earth. It gets into their minds and ways of life and finds its place at their tables, beds, and the community. Once it gets accepted as a way of life, a whole generation can be lost.

It was Dr. Myles Munroe who once famously said, *"Most people are poor because they do not know who they are!"* But I also know that there is no greater remedy for poverty than an enlightened mind coupled with a powerful spirit of hope, passion, and determination. These two forces can cut through the steel walls of poverty as a child will dismantle a spider's web. Knowledge and spirit, once put into action, can solve virtually any human problem around the world. I had the spirit, and I knew that I could not allow poverty to rob me of knowledge.

I stayed at home for two weeks, and by now, I am sure you already know what I was up to. All those two weeks, I never stopped crying and begging. Was that the seeking I was talking about? I do not know. But the cries were, again, the only weapon I had at that time. I let out my sorrows and lamentations daily. I could not just give up. I think I could never have taken anything in my life if I would not get an education. In my heart of hearts, I do not think I would have been any comfortable anywhere without an education. I was "pregnant" with that education baby, and I had to carry it full term. I was like a plane on a runway that was already at top speed, just about to take off. That plane could not be stopped. It had to fly.

After two weeks of weeping and crying over my life, my brother Samson could not handle the sorrow anymore. He acted. He borrowed some money enough to pay half of my school fees. Did you smell that? A breakthrough!

Again let me say, I could have given up at that moment, and even you would understand. And probably that would have been the end of my story, but I am not of those who draw back and give up on a dream!

I went back to Kangole Girls and was allowed to study by the administration. At the back of my brother's mind, I am sure he might have been asking himself, "How long will we keep up with this?" Mercy also came my way once more for I was allowed to stay at school to the end of the term without clearing the balance of the school fees.

Chapter 13

The Bite That Brought Respite

The second term was a special term for me and the school. Part of the promises I had made to the head teacher when I sought admission was that I was talented and would compete for the school. It was my opportunity to deliver on that promise.

I had an opportunity back at Arengesiep to prove to myself that indeed I was talented and gifted with fleet feet. When I did win the competition, it cemented in my mind the fact that I was blessed with pace. So now at Kangole, as I represented the school, I was not any bit surprised when I won. I was the very best.

Finally, I delivered what I had promised, and that again vindicated the head teacher's decision to give me admission at the school. I got several gifts at that time for that achievement. This must have softened the school administration to allow me to continue with my studies. Back then, schools would take such competitions seriously, and any girl who would put them on the map would be a treasure. I was christened Pajero. To date, all my former schoolmates at Kangole refer to me either as Our Pajero or Gazelle due to my blistering pace in short-distance races, especially in the one-hundred-meter and two-hundred-meter races.

One day, the school bursar noticed the big fees balance that I had and inquired of me. She asked, "Who pays your school fees?" I told her that I paid it myself. She was shocked. "How do you do that?" she pressed. "I brew malwa," I informed her. I am sure she had heard of such cases over and over again. She let me go on with my classes.

During that time, the school had organized a Scripture Union Conference. They invited a dynamic speaker to speak to us girls. For some reason, nearly everything he said touched on my life. It was as if someone had given him my life's script and he read it before coming to speak to us.

"Some of you in here are brewing in order to get school fees," he charged. "I want to pray for you so that God himself will provide for your fees without you having to engage in that vice." He asked those of us who were in that practice to approach the altar for prayer. I obliged. This was the Youth Alive program, as we would call it in those days. Soon after, the term closed, and I went back to my brother's place in Katakwi, honoring my own resolve not to go back to Amudat.

When third term came, I reported back to school in the same state as I did for the second term. I did not have school fees. I probably got favor with the school administration because of my excellence in class as well as my participation in athletics that gave the school a name in the district. I still operated on faith and refused to give up on my studies.

It so happened that one evening, as I left evening preps to go to the dormitory, an incident that totally changed my life took place. Such unrelated happenings have a way of connecting the dots of your life, yet at the time they take place, you may not realize it. A good example is when young David is tending his sheep and his dad "casually" sends him to take food to his big brothers. He could have refused to go. Yet what awaited David that day was a giant who would usher him to his eternal fame and world renown.

As for me, it was not as rosy a story as it was for David. As I passed through the shrubs on the way to the dormitory, I felt a seriously sharp pain on my leg. That pain could only be caused by either a scorpion bite or a snakebite. Up to that moment, I had never felt such a pain from a bite before. It was excruciating. I was shocked and scared and ran back to my class. I started narrating to my classmates what had just happened to me.

As usual, they thought that I was telling tales or making jokes, which was what I was fond of and was known for. I believed that that sting was caused by a snake, and I wanted to get a flashlight and go back to investigate. In a few moments, I blacked out and fainted! That was when they realized that I was telling the truth. I was rushed to the nearby dispensary and got admitted. This was anywhere between 9:00 p.m. and 10:00 p.m.

At the dispensary, they used the black-stone method on my leg to suck out the supposed poison. Soon after, I was released to go back to school. However, I was incapacitated for a few days or probably close to a week. I could not attend classes. This was the worst timing for that snakebite for I did not have any money to pay at the dispensary. In addition, no relative of mine came to visit even after I had that near-death experience. I believe that if the students had not acted fast enough to check me into the dispensary, I would have lost my life. Another close shave with death. I wonder why it was so relentlessly seeking to take me out all my life!

It was that situation I found myself in that attracted an angel into my life. The nun in charge of sports was curiously concerned about me. She called me and asked me, "Who are you? Do you have any parents who look after you? Where do you come from?" All these questions were prodding. It seemed to me like the nuns had all been alerted about my circumstances and they wanted to find out everything about me.

They must have had a discussion at the convent about a girl who was bitten by a snake and did not have any money to pay the dispensary and, at the same time, had school-fee arrears. So this nun took the trouble to find out. She called me and said, "I want to talk to you." I think this was the very first time in my life that I felt that someone outside of my family circles cared enough to want to hear about my short and miserable life.

I would have told the head teacher about my life when I came for admission at Kangole like I was just about to tell that nun. However, in the kingdom of God, timing is everything. I felt that at that point in time, it was now

91

appropriate to unload my baggage and heave down my burden to another human being so that they could see how heavy it had been for me. The fact is that I could have easily unburdened myself and stopped schooling; however, I envisaged that the burden of not schooling would have been greater than the burden of paying school fees. So that day, the floodgates of my tears were opened as I laid down my burden to the sister.

I told her everything about my miserable existence up to then. I told her how I had been bereaved of my dear father at a young age. I told her how my mother was destitute and not in a position to help me. I told her about my uncle who graciously took care of me but could no longer afford to do so. I told her about how I was abandoned in Amudat. I told her how I brewed malwa and waragi and paid for my own school fees. And then I went ahead and told her my greatest wish at that time—that someone would employ me as a potter so I could earn enough money to pay for all the arrears I had for school fees and on to completion.

As she sat there listening to my story, I could feel that she really *did* care. I could feel her heart connecting to the authenticity of the story, and I could feel the compassion. I think she must have cried too that day. For the very first time in my life, I had someone else in my life who cried because of my situation. And that day, her cry was not like mine. There are different types of cries. Hers was a cry of compassion; mine had always been cries of despair. Her cry opened up a door of possibilities for me—not just at that point in my life, but even later on after I was through with Kangole Girls Senior Secondary School.

Yes, if it was not for this angel of God, I do not know what my life could have turned out to be. You see, you may have knowledge and spirit, but the way God has structured this world is that we need people to bring our dreams to fruition. Sometimes, the people who matter in our lives are perfect strangers. In fact, the people who make great contributions in our lives are those who may not even be interested in getting a payback from us. Such people are moved by the spirit of compassion.

I have reason to believe that resources are not what move this world for the greater good. There are multiplied thousands of people who have resources but lack compassion. So such people deploy their resources on things that are temporal and visible, things that can be counted, things that are tangible and can guarantee a return. A famous quote is attributed to Albert Einstein that says, *"Not everything that counts can be counted, and not everything that can be counted counts."* And sometimes—in fact, most of the times—the things that cannot be counted are those that are of eternal value. Compassion is an infinite force. I dare say that if things are what are needed to change the world, then Jesus Christ would have come with gold and sapphires from heaven. Compassion also always finds a way where poverty has declared there is none. And for sure, the sister in her compassion did find a way for me.

She was so touched by my story. She said, "All along I didn't know that that was what you were going through in your life." She said she would talk to her fellow nuns to see if I could be included under the needy students' scheme. You cannot quantify my joy when I heard about this. And to think that probably this breakthrough was brought about by a snakebite is mind-boggling. Chances are that if I was not incapacitated by that snakebite, my story or predicament would not have come to the attention of the nuns.

Her name is Sister Susan Anyango from Tororo, the nun I spoke about earlier who answered the call to serve God. Finally, our unconnected paths had a meeting point, and from that moment on, she would play a massive role in my life, like the mother I never had! She must have made a great impression on the nuns for it was agreed that I would receive a bursary and have all my fees paid. Listen, we are talking about *my whole junior secondary education* fully sponsored for the rest of my stay at that school! This was the very first time that such a miracle took place in my life, and there I was, a few days before thinking I had only survived death!

The one who was miserable would no longer see the misery of lacking school fees, praise God! The one who knew only tears every time she was supposed to go back to school had now received salvation from none other than a perfect stranger! Would you believe that wonderful connection? People who say that there is no god will call that a coincidence, but I do not believe that things happen arbitrarily. I believe in purpose, that every single occurrence, however unrelated to anything it may seem, has a place and a reason on earth.

Sister Susan Anyango was born for such a time as this in my life. I believe that this was her purpose for existence and that she rose to be counted when it mattered. God knows that even today, and forevermore, I do not have words good enough to thank the Society of the Sacred Heart Sisters. If it was not for them and their organization, I am sure that my story would not have been pieced together. My story today might be a very remote and unrelated thing to some of the sisters, for they see very many cases like mine daily. To me, however, they are part and parcel of my history, more so Sister Susan Anyango from Tororo. Just pause and think about it: no more hustling for school fees. It felt like Jesus saying *"All debts paid in full"* as he hung on that cross, dying for the sins of humanity. Who can repay such benevolence?

As for me, there had to be something that I could do to show appreciation. My clan and indeed my tribe have a deep norm of always giving back to the hand that feeds you. Besides my school fees being paid, I also needed some subsistence supplies such as clothes, soap, sugar, and the normal things that make life easier for a student at school. I realized that you could volunteer to work for such things in the school vicinity.

That term, I worked for a whole month and three weeks. That included digging, fetching water, slashing the school compound, cleaning the convent, weeding, and so on. The school would actually provide sanctuary to some kids who were disadvantaged to stay on over the holidays. In turn, they would volunteer to do some common tasks during the holidays. This, again, was another laudable move by the organization. It taught us the value of hard work, discipline, and maturity. Honestly, the person I am today is a result of what I learned during that time, even though I volunteered myself.

The most tedious of it was digging. Karamoja is a very hard place with very tough ground. On numerous occasions, the very hoes that we would use to dig would get broken by virtue of the hard terrain. I can still remember one day when I was told to dig up a rubbish pit. I was told that for it to be a pit, it should be big enough to swallow me.

There was a term when we spent our holidays ferrying sand from the river using our Pajero. We would load it in the lorry and off-load it.

Now, someone might take pity on me at that point in time, but I was having a blast. That was one of the best times in my life. No longer would I be burdened by school fees. No longer would my studies be interrupted. Besides, every single day, they gave us food to eat during and after work. It was bliss, I tell you!

So Betty Ogiel dug for her future. I had cried for my future previously and moved on. I am not so sure if there was still room for that option anymore. Also, I had to run for my future. It was not a normal childhood. Then I had brewed for my future. I also had to smuggle for my future. Now I was digging for my future.

My destiny seems to be hidden in very awkward things! At least that was progress. I was not stuck anymore, you could say. Whereas the goal remained the same, the methods of getting there were changing, and I was adapting as we moved along. At least, it would be one year closer to the dream, and that year would not be a year of despair. Thank God! When I hear comments from people saying, "I wish I had more people like you" or "I wish I could clone you," they have no idea that I began working early on. My past made me have a strong work ethic. For me, in my own way, I knew that the only way to come out of poverty was through school.

Marriage was the remotest option for me. The dating life was a no-no for me. It was a pure waste of time. I saw boys as distractions, and I would fight them off. In fact, that was one of the reasons I did not want to go back to Amudat, because the boys were waiting for me to beat me up. I had also seen how the married people were suffering. My own mother, a peasant, was left with seven young children. The plan for her to give birth and for my father to take care of us had backfired on her. Now she had a burden that was beyond her means to carry. She had not even seen a blackboard.

I never wanted to be like my mother. I wanted to be different and not struggle. Then about marriage, I saw how my uncle was beating his wife. That discouraged me. I even grew up with a big bias about men. That biasness affected my first relationship. I had no respect for men because of what I had grown up seeing, until I gave my life to Christ and understood maturity in faith.

So I worked all the way up to senior 4. The least amount of time I would go home for holidays was one week just before the term reopened. So you could say that I literally transferred from home to school nearly on a full-time basis for a full three years!

Looking back and honestly speaking, I think it was good. It made me who I am today. If I had an easy bursary, probably I could have taken things for granted, although at that time, I would have loved to have had the bursary. I am a person who did not know English, even one word of English. I was just brought from the village and thrust directly to primary 1, where the mode of instruction was English and Swahili, languages I did not even know. But I learned Swahili so fast and became a pro in it. I also learned the Pokot language. I used to admire people who spoke in English, and I used to want to be like them. I knew that if I had to be like them, I had to study. That was right from the beginning. I was among the best in class. About English, by the time I left primary, I would both read and write English without a problem.

Kangole Girls, you will forever be in my heart, fondly remembered. It was good, and it was real. I am forever grateful.

In a special way, I would love to end this chapter by honoring the founders, the workers, the administration, and the vision bearers of the Society of the Sacred Heart. This book is dedicated to you. I need you to know that your efforts paid off. I need to also encourage you to keep doing what you have been called to do. Words are not good enough for this once-destitute orphan to ever say *thank you*. My late father would tell you, *"Eyalama noi."* All my Karamojong friends would tell you, *"Alakara noi."* Thank you. I am a life that was changed by your giving. Thank you.

Chapter 14

The Man I Wish I Knew

It was a beautiful Monday morning. The sun was out over Eastern Uganda. The atmosphere was calm, permeated by fresh air in my rural home in Katakwi. The clouds were already out and showing the signs that it would soon rain. People went about their activities trying to eke out a living.

That was the place I had left more than twelve years back. I was back to where it all began. That was where a certain young man by the name of Samson Icaraat was born. He was the firstborn among four siblings: three boys and a girl. He grew up in stature and in intelligence unrivaled in the clan. Certainly, everyone who interacted with him noticed that there was something special about him. People perceived that he would have a big future. His parents decided to take him to school as with his siblings when they did come along. He proved himself to be so witty at school, and soon enough, he had an opportunity to go to further his studies in senior 5 and 6.

By that time, his brother Nicholas was also in school and very promising. One day, his parents called Samson aside and asked to have a discussion with him. In those days, a meeting with parents was a serious matter. They were concerned about the estate of the family and their future. They did not have enough money to take all the kids to school. Samson was asked to make a decision on whether his parents should continue sponsoring his education at the expense of his younger brother Nicholas. In that case, Nicholas would remain at home and take care of the homestead. In turn, Samson, once successful with his schooling and employed (it was relatively easy to get employment in those days after successfully finishing school, especially with the government), would be supporting the family by sending back some monies.

It was a tough decision. Samson did the most benevolent of things—he gave up his opportunity to further his studies so that his younger brother Nicholas could take the chance. That decision would be life changing to both boys in ways that no one would have expected later on. Once the decision was made, it was now incumbent upon Samson to take up the responsibility of being the head of the home. That, of course, meant that he had to get married.

About two kilometers away, there was a family that Samson's dad was a friend to. They had a beautiful daughter who was responsible. In those days, a good woman was one who was well-behaved and could take care of the family. Education was not considered like it is nowadays. There was no major ceremony held as Samson got married and started his own family. Meanwhile, his brother Nicholas continued with his studies. He too was bright, and there were good prospects for him. The family was averagely doing well.

One day, while in his early thirties, Samson was appointed by the government of the day as a subparish chief. This was a major breakthrough for him to start working with the government. It also meant that he would receive military training from the government before being officially installed. Once successful, Samson would always put on his official regalia, which was some kind of military or police fatigue. He was respected, and his parents felt so proud of him. The clansmen also loved him so much and were fond of him.

In the meantime, his own family started growing as his wife blessed him with children. Everything looked well on course and maybe even beyond his dreams. Apart from being a subparish chief, Samson was also a farmer. He grew sorghum, millet, cassava, and bananas. He was mainly a subsistence farmer, and the excess produce he got would be sold at the village market.

Samson was a great leader, even though that was the least position in rank with the government leadership hierarchy. His superiors also saw his wit, courage, eloquence, and intelligence and marked him for greater things. He was so close to his siblings as well as his family. He was an upright man who spoke with authority and commanded an air of certainty around him.

At some point in time, the government needed to appoint a subcounty chief. For this to happen, an official examination had to be done, and Samson was extended the offer. This was unprecedented because the position to be filled was two scales higher than his current position. This meant that Samson would actually skip one position (parish chief) and land straight to the subcounty position.

Indeed, after the tests were done, it was none other than Samson that was earmarked for that position. When the news of this breakthrough was received, the people in the clan were so very happy. Congratulatory messages were received at the home of Samson's parents over and over again as people came visiting to pledge their allegiance and show their pride in this feat.

Nicholas had just come back from holidays in school. The two of them were very close. Samson always encouraged Nicholas to study hard and be the best. He cherished very much the idea of people studying, and he wanted Nicholas to take his chances seriously. Nicholas, in turn, looked at his elder brother with so much awe and adoration. He was proud to be a brother to the next subcounty chief. That position in today's ranks is equivalent to a chief administrative officer, perhaps even greater. The family was now on track to experiencing prosperity. Samson's wife was so proud of him. She also knew that she had married well. She knew that her children would never lack as compared to other families she saw struggling in the clan.

Samson's area of jurisdiction was in Katakwi. At some point in time, he had to move his family from that location due to the constant raids conducted by the Karamojong warriors. The family finally settled in Serere. However,

Samson would commute between Katakwi and Serere in order to fulfill his duties as the subparish chief.

Before he was installed as the subcounty chief, Samson was in his regular routine back to Serere from Katakwi one day. However, he needed to eat before he could proceed back home to Serere. He got into a new restaurant at Katakwi and ordered for his favorite meal. Once he finished eating his meal, he set off to his family in Serere.

Immediately, as he arrived home, he felt such a sharp pain in his stomach. That was unlike something he had ever experienced before. He turned to his wife and started complaining about it. As the pain increased, suddenly, Samson started asking himself questions about the origin of this stomach "disease." As he traced his steps that day, he realized that as he was eating at Katakwi, there was something unusual about the looks of the people that served him. He came to the conclusion that someone must have poisoned him.

Samson turned to his dear wife and, with a knowing that was beyond argument, told her, "They have killed me. Please, please do take care of my children." At that time, Samson's wife was nursing a one-year-old baby, the sixth born. Her elder sister Betty was about three years old. Samson's wife mobilized resources and rushed him to the nearest hospital in Soroti, which was more than twenty-five kilometers away.

By the time they got to the hospital, Samson, according to his wife, had vomited his gut out, literally. The alleged poison that he was given had literally crushed his intestines into a muddy mess. Samson died a horrible and painful death within five hours of being poisoned. A young life was ruthlessly plucked out of the earth at a very promising and tender age of only forty-one years old.

The news about Samson being rushed to the hospital hit Nicholas as he arrived home that day. He decided that he would go see his dear brother the very next day due to the unavailability of means of transportation. The following day, as Nicholas was heading toward Soroti, he met a relative who was coming from the hospital. The relative could not hold back her grief, and she broke down in a piercing shriek and wails. Nicholas right then and there realized what had happened.

Grief was something he had never known in his life. That day, he knew how sickening it tasted. It felt as if this uncontrollable sorrow and pain of the spirit overcame him. Waves upon waves of heartache, pain, and sorrow overwhelmed him as he had no strength to continue standing.

When the news about Samson's demise got to his family and the clan at large, there was pandemonium. There had never been such a great outcry in the clan like this for a long while. Many people loved Samson. He was healthy. Some had even interacted with him just a few days prior to his untimely death. This was one of the biggest shockers of the clan at that time. How could he die just like that? Oh, what a promise he had!

Funeral arrangements were made. And as Samson's family gathered beside his freshly dug grave, a three-year-old girl was beside her mother, totally oblivious of what was happening. Each family member was given some soil in order to "bury" their loved one by throwing it into the grave. The three-year-old girl was me. Uncle Nicholas told me that I did not throw in the soil as was expected of me, but I put it in my mouth and ate it! Well, I do not remember those details at all.

Shortly after, Uncle Nicholas was given the responsibility of taking care of my family by the clan. He was actually supposed to take over his brother's house by marrying my mother and take care of all of us. At that time, Uncle Nicholas was at a teachers' training college and was not in the position to get married. Three years later, he sent a message to my mother requesting that she take me to him. He knew that I was now at a school-going age. Mom was happy. She took me to Katakwi, where we met Uncle Nicholas, who was true to his word. He took me with him to Amudat, where he had been posted as a trained primary school teacher.

Chapter 15

Which Way Now?

So that beautiful Monday morning, that teenage girl realized that the highest level of education that had been attained in her own immediate family was senior 4, and that was by her late father. That was exactly where she had reached against all odds herself. On finishing our exams, there was no staying in school anymore to work, as had been the custom for me.

My mother had requested my brother to take me to Serere immediately after I finished school. She had a plan for me, to link me up with a cousin who worked at the District Farm Institute (DFI). In her thinking, he would give me a job. My cousin was the principal of District Farm Institute.

Once I got there, I put up with a cousin-brother of mine as I awaited the position. I was a very outgoing person and quickly made friends with a girl called Sharon Akioto, who was also on senior 4 vacation. All senior 4 "vacists" would have a lot of time at home awaiting the Uganda National Examinations Board (UNEB) results that would determine what next: either to go the advanced level of education (senior 5 and 6) or to get admission to colleges for courses leading to the award of diplomas or certificates.

Sharon was already working as a casual laborer for Serere Agricultural Research Institute (SARI), and we would spend some time talking. We became so fond of each other, such good friends. Meanwhile, my cousin-brother kept promising me over and over again that he would get me to the casual-laborers list, but it never materialized. I had been accustomed to working all my life up to then, and that was all I wanted to do at that moment. I knew I was hardworking. I also knew that working came with work benefits, such as wages that I would save for future use. I was so hungry to work.

At that point in time, for the very first time in my life, I gave up on school. Sister Susan was no longer in the country. She had gone to India for further studies. She was my only hope that I had at that time. I knew when I stepped out of Kangole Girls that that would be the end of my education. So I gave up. We, however, kept in touch through writing letters to each other. When I got to Serere, I wrote to her, informing her of my new postal address.

One day, Sharon came to me with very pleasant news. Her father had called her to Kampala, the capital city of the country, and she really wanted me to replace her at the place of work. I was beyond excited. However, there was one hurdle: it was not up to her to decide who worked in her stead. It was up to her supervisor. One thing about me is that God has given me lots of confidence. If I needed something from someone, I could approach them without much fear. I could speak for myself. This started early in those days of brewing malwa for my school fees when I approached that lady who introduced me to smuggling local brew to Kenya. I had the confidence to represent myself and get an admission at Kangole Girls. This was not a new thing.

So the both of us approached my friend's supervisor, and after she had explained her absence from work, I took over and sold my credentials to the supervisor. Fortunately for me, he took me and assigned me her responsibilities at SARI, which was adjacent to DFI. That was another first in the life of Betty Ogiel. I had personally negotiated to start working officially! I was over the moon when this happened, and I decided to give it the very best that I could muster.

I worked hard picking cotton from the SARI gardens. All the monies that we would be paid, I would not use. We were paid 3,600 Uganda shillings weekly. Somehow I had learned the discipline of saving. I kept nearly all that money since there were negligible expenses on me. I was staying with my cousin, and there was no need to pay rent or spend money buying food. At that time, the bug of entrepreneurship bit me also. At the institute, there were trainings being carried on occasionally. I figured that I could work with the food provider as a caterer during those training moments.

I approached my cousin and mooted the idea to him, and after he gave me the green light, I delved into action. I had cried for my future, smuggled for my future, brewed for my future, dug for my future, and now it was time for me to pluck and cook for my future! All the proceeds that came out of plucking cotton and cooking for the trainees I would give to my cousin to keep for me. I was also good at knitting; I made tablecloths for several people and sold those to them at a fee. I could knit throughout the night, making tablecloths to deliver as ordered. I never "ate" the money. I saved it all.

Eventually, the results of senior 4 national examinations came out. I had performed relatively well, coming out with a grade of 2. But I had given up on school. I honestly did not have enough emotional energy to fight for my time in school anymore. I was simply weary. With Sister Susan out of the picture, I couldn't bring myself to fight for my education anymore. I felt overwhelmed. Besides, I was already working and making some money. This, however, was a casual and temporary thing. I longed for a permanent job.

After a moment of reflection, I figured that I could become a police officer. At that time, I had also made friends with another girl at the institute. I convinced her about the aspect of becoming police officers. That is how good I was with my negotiating skills. I remember that after I had successfully convinced her, she asked, "But how do we get recruited?" I told her we just have to go to the police station and ask. So one day, we made our journey, armed with our result slips from our schools, to the nearest police post. The plan was fully in motion. But we were green and naive. The police post was about four kilometers away, and so we went on bipedally there.

106

Something funny happened when we got at the gate. We were just about to enter the station compound when a stranger confronted us with questions. "What are you girls doing here?" he quipped. "What problem do you have that you are going into the police station? Are you pregnant?" he insisted. We found it so funny since pregnancy would have been the last thing on our minds at that time. So we laughed it off and explained to him what was happening to us. We told him that we were stuck and could not continue with our education. We told him that we thought the next logical step would be to join the police force.

He was taken aback and amazed when he realized how serious we were! Then he told us how tough it was to get into the police force. He told us how he tried it himself but that the training was so rigorous that he dropped out. When he looked at us, he did not think that we would make it. He asked to see our result slips. He took one glance at my results and exclaimed, "You have very good grades. Don't you know that you could receive admission at Ngora High School if you went and talked to them?"

From out of the blue, a stranger had given me another intangible but eternal resource: hope. Once he said that, I knew I could not settle down. The bug had bitten me, and now I was again pregnant with the hunger to study. I knew that there was now a possibility to go study for my senior 5 and senior 6 levels under the school's sports bursary. This was something that I had already given up on. It seems to me that life was kind of giving back to me. It would not let me give up, and so in its own unique way, it gave me a chance through a stranger!

I will say it again: sometimes in life, strangers offer the most potent help and connection toward our predetermined destinies! We quickly abandoned the police mission and went back home to picking cotton at the institute. Days later, I approached Peter, my eldest brother, and asked him if he could help me secure admission at Ngora High School for my advanced levels. I loved the school because it was of high standards. Much as I did not have enough money to pay for my school fees, I was never drawn to schools of below-par standards in my estimation. I had tested one of them in senior 1, and there was no way I would look forward to that kind of school anymore.

My brother and I embarked on an approximately forty-kilometer bipedal journey to Ngora High School. When we got there, I did all the talking. Peter could not communicate in English. I negotiated with them, and we went back home having great prospects of getting an admission. I had made sure that I talked to the games teacher, leveraging not just my pass marks but also my gift and talent in athletics.

Soon enough, we would know our fate, and for sure, I got the admission! I was back in business! There was no hesitancy with taking up the admission by virtue of not having school fees as I had been piling up all my wages. My brother too was willing to sell his cow to add up to whatever monies I had. You can say I was cruising, and to think that just a few weeks back, I had given up and was looking forward to be a police officer!

It is true. Sometimes we give up when we are just about to get to our breakthroughs. I think the lesson for me is to always check myself at those moments that I am just about to give up. I can be just about to enter into another level. This situation is captured in an all-time classic book called *Acres of Diamonds*. We give up on our diamonds and go seek something else outside of what we have, not knowing that all along what we are leaving is what we have been looking for.

I think we also do need mentors in our lives, especially when we get to those crucial moments of transitions at certain junctures of our existence. Such moments are so precarious. At times, it is like we are standing at the proverbial fork in the road with only two directions to choose from. Our choice at that point needs to be directed by a mentor, someone who sees beyond what we can see ourselves, someone who has experience, and someone who loves us and truly cares about us. Very many children the world over lack such a person in their lives.

For me, God sent another random angel in the name of that stranger who stopped us at the gate of the police station. Come to think of it, what business did he have talking to two girls who were strangers to him? None. But he, in that brief exchange that I think lasted not more than five minutes, mentored me and opened for me a door for my life. That fact is beyond amazing. It is simply divine. We made all the preparations necessary to join Ngora High School. I did all the shopping that I needed to do. I had all the school necessities purchased, locked and loaded, and ready to go.

Speaking of the Divine, while all this was happening, unbeknownst to me, Sister Susan Anyango was back in the country. She had been posted at a school in Masaka, hundreds of kilometers from Serere. Naturally, she found out that I had passed my senior 4 examinations, and she went ahead and started organizing my next move in life! She still remembered me and actually tracked me down through mail. I had sent her our latest post-office address. You can imagine my pleasant surprise when I got a missive from her.

Now, this letter was not just any type of letter. It brought good tidings with it. This letter actually was received a day before I was supposed to report to Ngora High School. Sister Susan was inviting me to Masaka, where she was stationed at a convent there. She wanted me to continue with my studies under her care.

For the very first time in my life, I had to make a decision over two options that both seemed good. Remember, I loved Ngora High because of their standards. I also knew that wherever Sister Susan was, the school had very high standards just like Kangole Girls, or maybe even better, since they were under the same administration of the Society of the Sacred Heart Sisters. Faith came into application once again as I chose to go to Masaka. Now, mark you that I had never been to Kampala before, let alone Masaka. To go to Masaka, one had to pass through Kampala, the capital city of the country. The only time I was in Kampala was at night, and we just passed through it on our way to Western Uganda for sports! Now, I had to make it to Masaka all by myself. Well, I had done pretty many things all by myself.

As the excitement boiled, I embarked on the journey that would introduce me to a pretty new environment in my life. All my life I had spent in Northeastern Uganda. Now, it was an opportunity to move and experience life in Central Uganda. I was up for it.

Chapter 16

One Step Ahead

Since everything I needed for school had already been prepared, I traveled alone to Kampala with my luggage and metallic box. I got to the bus park at 10:00 a.m. Sister Susan had given me instructions on how to locate the convent. The convent was not in Masaka exactly but some kilometers away from it, a place called Kalungu. I was to travel to Masaka via a place called Nyendo in order to access Kalungu. Once in Nyendo, I would decide to use either a taxi or a motorbike ride to get to the convent. I decided on the latter because they would drop me smack at the gate of the convent.

All this was a dream. It was a pleasant reunion with Sister Susan when she saw me at the gate. She must have been waiting for me all those days. You know, back then, we did not have cell phones to call and locate. We operated blindly, so to speak, but the world still moved in strides. We hugged each other and exchanged niceties before Sister Susan dropped a bomb on me: I was not assured of admission at the school! I had to sit for entry examinations before I could be accepted! This meant that there was a possibility of failing and going back to Serere.

My heart skipped several beats. Must life have to tempt me at every corner? Was life conspiring to stop my progress by all means possible? The fact that Sister Susan was part of the school administration did not have any bearing on my chances there. If I did not pass the examinations, I would not be admitted. The head teacher was known to be extra strict. Actually, there was a sister to a priest well-known to the nuns at the convent. She was one of my classmates back at Kangole. The priest was friends to the headmistress, but when his sister failed the entry examinations, she was sent away. When I was told about this story, my heart sank. I could not imagine myself carrying my luggage in shame, heading back to Serere. But thanks be to God! After sitting for that interview, I aced it and was immediately admitted to the school.

It was amazing. All the while I was planning on giving up with my education, a stranger, or let me say an angel of God, was busy scheming by all means possible to make sure that I pursued my schooling. Sometimes we never know what the Divine has in store for us. Sometimes we think that we have been forgotten and our lights snuffed out. Sometimes we think that our fight against what enslaves us has been totally lost. And sometimes we think that life is cruel enough to give us a glimmer of hope, only to extinguish it out. Rosa Parks must have thought so. Martin Luther King must have thought so too. Peter, James, and John, the three friends of Jesus, must have gone through the same thing when they saw whom they thought was their lord and savior hanging on a cross, crucified for nothing done against humanity. Having watched him perform miracle after miracle, they thought he would overcome this obstacle. But as the entrance of the tomb was sealed, their hopes evaporated. Actually, Peter and his friends went back fishing. They must have said, "It was good while it lasted. Now let's face reality." But of course, the reality was interrupted once again by the divine purpose.

Purpose never dies no matter the levels of opposition it faces. I had given up on it, but it had not given up on me. It was alive and well. Sometimes we fight for our purpose and destiny, and sometimes when we have given up, it fights for us and brings us up again until it is accomplished. I had my money for the first term. I paid in full all the necessary fees that were needed for the first term. It was another opportunity to feel proud of myself for catering to all my expenses at school for the first term.

Learning began in earnest. Just as it was at Kangole Girls, I was among the top five girls at St. Charles Lwanga Girls Training Center–Kalungu, popularly known as Kalungu GTC all through my stay there. God had given me two wings to fly: one wing was through athletics, and the other one was through academics. They were such rare gifts to find, yet these very gifts faced the prospect of staying obscure and never coming to the fore by virtue of the scourge of poverty. My determination and resilience thawed away the claws of poverty one finger at a time. At times, that is what is needed to fight poverty. I am convinced that when we stand up and focus on defeating the tentacles of poverty and are relentless and determined, sooner or later, that scourge will be mastered, defeated, and locked away.

I tell you once again, poverty is a liar. And as I went back home for the first-term holidays, sure enough, poverty was there to welcome me. I could no longer rely on my temporary job as a casual laborer because the holiday period was not as extended for us. Time came to go back to school, and as the previous numerous occasions, there was no money to send me to school. Uncle Nicholas was out of the picture because he was also paying school fees for two of my cousins, let alone taking care of his own immediate family.

At times, as a girl-child, you get so many disadvantages, especially back then. As much as your folks do love and care about you, as a girl-child, your education is not necessarily a priority. Education for the boys comes first. Marital obligations also supersede the education of a girl-child. That is why one of my brothers could afford to take care of his dowry negotiations at the same time that I needed school fees to go back to Kangole Girls for the second term a few years earlier. Thank God for Sister Susan. When all my hope seemed lost, after staying at home for one week, I wrote to her and informed her of my predicament. Another thing that we need to realize is that asking for help is also a strong character. It is not easy to always ask the same person for help over and over again. We have an internal sense of pride that gets wounded when we appear helpless before another human being. However, I had to overcome this self-imposed stereotype in order to forge ahead with my education. On the other hand, there are other human beings who understand the exact thing that I have just described. They have grace about them when they are offering you help. And this is what Sister Susan brought into my life.

Up to today, I have no idea where I would have been without that God-sent angel. Once again, the Society of the Sacred Heart as an organization must be lauded for the great work that they have done to give their lives to serve humanity. There are countless girls and boys around the world whose lives have totally changed for the better because of the sacrifice of these nuns. I am just one girl-child that has been touched and blessed by their sacrifice. However, even if it may seem that this help and sacrifice are an obvious call to duty, there are some special people who still take it a notch higher.

Sister Susan is one such person. So when I informed her of my predicament, she asked me to find some means to get back to school so she would be able to sort out my school-fee conundrum. My brother helped me get bus fare all the way to Kalungu GTC, and when I got there, my angel, Sister Susan, was on hand to receive me. She talked to the school administration and informed them of my setbacks. She asked that I be included in the list of the needy students whose fees were being catered to by the convent's solidarity fund. My case was special because this scheme was not open past the level of senior 4. However, there has always been an exception to the rule, and I believe such has been the case of my entire life.

Poverty said it would shove me down the same way it did for my mother. It started with my siblings and systematically made sure that none of them would go past senior 4, the level that our dad had attained. But I was the exception to the rule through determination, resilience, and the contribution from the Divine to meet me halfway. As it was in Kangole, I knew the closest I could get to repaying this benevolence was through volunteering to work. However, this was less tedious as compared to Kangole Girls in Karamoja. The terrain was softer and more palatable. Second, I only worked on Saturdays, and the work was task based. This meant that I would be given specific tasks, and once completed, that would be the end of it. Some of these tasks involved pumping water, slashing, and cleaning.

One incident comes to mind, though. There were particular people back at Kalungu GTC and Kangole Girls who did not like me at all. This is the nature of life anyway; you cannot impress everybody. One day, one of them found me slashing on a Saturday morning and started lording it over me, accusing me, shouting at me and quarreling, creating a massive fuss over nothing serious in particular. I had not done anything wrong to deserve the treatment that they were giving me.

At that very young age, my heart discerned that authority was being misused here. It felt as if they knew how sorry my state was, and they were using their authority to intimidate me. That day, I went back to my dormitory and cried heavy and hot tears. I recorded in my diary that day, as tears blinded my eyes and soaked the pages of my diary, *"Poverty is a bad thing. I never applied to be poor."* Thoughts of my life's suffering back in Amudat working for school fees came back to me at that moment. I realized more of what and whom I did not have, and I temporarily forgot the blessedness of having all my school fees paid off all the way to senior 6.

Apart from that small incident, life at Kalungu GTC settled down for me well. It proved to be one of the most fruitful years of my life, those two years in senior 5 and senior 6. There were absolutely no more hassles with school fees. In turn, I gave out the very best that God had given me: intellect and prowess in athletics. I represented the school all the way up to the national levels. Although I never really made it to win at the national levels, I was always the best at the district level. All the while as I represented all the districts in which I schooled as their star, they started calling me Gazelle. This was a variation of what I was called at Kangole Girls where they referred to me as Our Pajero. I was *that* gifted.

However, I did not have a coach to help me through. I could just appear on the material day of the competition and run. I think the best I ever attained at the national level was position 2. Coaching and special training would have been important because the extracurricular-activity participation would earn you some good points that would increase your chances of getting a scholarship by the government. I am so convinced that my name would be up there at the nationals if I had a good trainer and a coach. I just expended my raw talent.

My academic performance was also good. When I did the interview at Kalungu GTC, I knew that I wanted to major in history, economics, and divinity. I would have done art as an additional subject, but that was a very expensive subject for a needy girl like me. There was never a time that I was not among the top five girls in my stream for those two years. I was blessed with great intelligence. My economics teacher would refer my colleagues to me. "Go to Betty and ask her. She knows these things," he would say. This was pure bliss for me. I had broken the curse in our family, and for the very first time since creation, a member of my clan was able to study all the way up to senior 6. The extent of the broken curse was so massive in that against all the odds in our society, the one who broke this curse was none other than me, a girl-child! Probably I did not consciously know the extent to which I had managed to break all the stereotypes that I was facing at that time in order to get an education.

In the midst of the Teso Insurgency between 1986 and 1991, the whole region was a no-go zone. I have already talked about the Karamojong warriors and the difficult terrain in the northeastern region where I was raised. I have already alluded to the fact that in my day and in the days of our fathers, a girl-child was never a priority in terms of education. However, for me, the death of my father and the subsequent suffering of my mother in raising us pinched my heart and opened my eyes. I realized that if I would not get an education, then the curse of poverty would continue operating in my life. I hated poverty with all my gut.

So being at Kalungu GTC at the top of my classes and also at the top of my game in athletics was a major testament for me. In fact, one of the highlights of my stay in Kalungu GTC came on the day when the Buganda Kingdom had a massive celebration for their *kabaka* (king). These celebrations were held in Masaka, just within reach off our school. The kingdom organized several sporting activities, and as the athletics queen of the district, I represented the school in short-distance races. As usual, I won each competition that I participated in and had the great honor of shaking the hand of the kabaka while standing. Culturally, you are not supposed to stand before the kabaka. In fact, some people lie on the ground as a sign of respect while the kabaka walks on them. I shook his hands as he gave me gifts for my achievements. The competition was sponsored by Uganda Breweries, and one of the presents I got for my winning the competition was a Bell T-shirt. Bell is a beer brand of Uganda Breweries. That T-shirt became one of my favorites, and I wore it so proudly.

That was a girl who had come against all odds to achieve the impossible. The Bible is so emphatic, and in the book of Proverbs, it states, *"Do you see a man diligent in his business? He shall stand before Kings; he shall not stand before obscure men."*[2] The word *diligent* is my second name right from the word *go.*

I remember in my days at Amudat, Uncle lived in a semipermanent house. The walls were made of mud, and the roof was made of iron sheets. I was so diligent in keeping that house smart in that it was the smartest house in the vicinity. I was also very creative in that I would mix ash and different clay soils to create beautiful paint that I would smear in different designs on the walls of that house. People admired it. The spirit of diligence was part of my DNA from a young age, and now it was beginning to pay off. The Bible still goes ahead to declare, *"A man's gift makes room for him and brings him before great men."*[3] There I was, focusing on my natural gift in athletics, and that gift alone made me stand before one of the greatest kings in Uganda.

---

[2]   Proverbs 22:29

[3]   Proverbs 18:16

However, I believe that the gift alone was not enough. It needed diligence. God had given me the gift as a seed, and through diligence, I had cultivated it to the best of my ability. I had refused to give up even going against hope itself. Through it all, I learned that connecting the dots of your life has two parts: the Divine and the self. I realized that the Divine is always activated by the self, and when the self does nothing for the most part, the Divine remains inactivated. The Divine is represented at times by common people and at times by strangers.

My brother, for example, sold the only cow he had so that I could attend school. Uncle Nicholas took it upon himself to educate me even though girl-child education was not the priority back then. The teachers noticed my gift in athletics at the time that I was totally oblivious to it. Sister Susan believed in my future and took it upon herself to educate this strange girl, knowing that she stood no chance in the present world to get her reward for her actions. They say that it takes a village to educate a child, but in my days, it takes a village to raise a girl-child to be a good childbearing wife.

By God's providence, I came through it all and sat for my final exams for the advanced level. I cried for my future. I smuggled for my future. I ran for my future. I brewed malwa for my future. I dug trenches for my future. I picked cotton for my future. I cooked for my future. I knitted for my future. I pumped water for my future. And now as my days at Kalungu GTC came to a close, time would tell if all my efforts had paid off.

Part 4

A New Frontier

Chapter 17

No Random Chance

Professor Epelu-Opio had formed a rigorous routine that he followed to the letter in order to keep up with his responsibilities. He is one of the luminaries in academia that had come from the Teso Subregion. The humble professor could easily be in the same generation as my parents. During their time, education was not a priority, not even for the boys. If you look at many African communities, you will realize that we are just a few generations away from the "bush," and that is a fact. Professor Epelu-Opio came from a blended family, having several mothers in a polygamous home. He is the second-last born of ten siblings—five boys and five girls. All his sisters never pursued any kind of formal education—not because of lack of resources, but generally because that was not the norm in the traditional African society where he lived at that time.

From his clan, it is only he and two other cousins who took education seriously. To date, the three of them are one of the most notable members of society not only in the Teso Subregion but also in the whole country of Uganda. After finishing his ordinary-level education, young Epelu-Opio's father wanted him to stop there and branch into one of the following options: prisons, police, or administration. During those days, the route to work was more plausible with those options and with that type of education level. This, however, was not on young Epelu-Opio's mind. He was determined to proceed as far as possible with his studies.

Lacking school fees, he quickly crafted the most plausible way of raising money: brewing. Although he did not know how to handle the whole process, he got someone who helped him with distilling it, and after a successful job, young Epelu-Opio had twenty-five shillings in his pocket. He walked up to his dad and told him that he would be leaving for school at a particular date and that he had the money for it.

On the material day, young Epelu-Opio traveled for the very first time from his hometown in Katakwi to Kampala. This was about the time that a certain Samson Icaraat was pondering the issues related to his future life and what direction he would take.

After young Epelu-Opio got admission in school, the District Education Office gave him a scholarship, and that was how he cleared his A level education, but he was not finished studying yet! Such hunger back in the sixties was a rare phenomenon.

His pursuits took him to Kenya, where he studied in the prestigious University of Nairobi, earning himself a degree in veterinary medicine. Shortly after this feat, he pursued a master's degree at the same institution and excelled. The humble professor came back to Uganda in 1973 and joined Makerere University for work.

At that time, my beloved father was still alive and well and was the local subparish chief in Katakwi. The political climate in Uganda in those days was rather unstable. In 1976, the professor decided to go to Zambia to work there and at the same time seek safety from the uncertainty of the political environment in Uganda. He came back to Uganda in 1980 for a brief holiday before going back to Zambia on a new contract. This was a brief stint that had to be cut short.

Professor Epelu-Opio's children were not comfortable in Zambia. They missed their homeland. So they kept entreating him to come back. He tried to reason with them about the political uncertainties in Uganda, but they prevailed upon him, and the whole family relocated back to Kampala. He joined the College of Veterinary Medicine at Makerere University, where his star shined and he became the head of that department in 1985. This was the very same time that I was facing all manner of odds, not even knowing where my life was leading. I did not know good from bad; I just existed where I had been born.

At that very time, Uncle Nicholas was preparing to launch me into the world of education, a decision that has shaped all my life. Had Uncle Nicholas not taken me to school, I am not so sure that you would be reading this script. You see, as human beings, we can only see today. We do not have the capacity to see in the future, much as motivational speakers insist that we need to visualize. I love the act of visualizing, but in comparison to really knowing how the future will be like, it pales in the shadow. That is where, I believe, God Almighty and the Divine comes in.

I am sure that before Professor Epelu-Opio was born, his life path had already been chartered by God himself. The paths of lives that would intersect with his during his lifetime were already mapped; he was just rehearsing it through. He came through odds himself. His education might not even have been deliberate, at least from his father's angle, but his divine assignment had already been chartered by God.

By 1985, our stories were so far apart that there was absolutely no way you could connect them. I believe no human being could easily connect my path to that of the humble professor—it had to be the work of the Divine.

In 1986, Yoweri Kaguta Museveni overthrew the sitting government and was sworn in as the president of the Republic of Uganda, giving his famous speech about fundamental change. At that time, he said, *"Nobody is to think that what is happening today, what has been happening in the last few days is a mere change of guards. . . . This is not a mere change of guards. I think this is a fundamental change in the politics of our government."*

As President Museveni was taking over power, the vanquished forces of the former president Tito Okello beat a hasty retreat. They were concentrated mainly in the Teso Subregion. During that time, they killed people as they fled from the National Resistance Army. One man who was unfortunate to lose his life in 1986 was none other than the biological father of Sister Susan Anyango.

However, in the ensuing years between the late eighties and the early nineties, the northeastern region of Uganda was encumbered with a terrible insurgence, popularly known as the Teso Insurgency. As rebel groups were fighting the government of the day, it was the people who suffered. The already impoverished people in the Teso Subregion were severely affected by that insurgency. The rebels believed in a special sheep as their "leader." Wherever and whenever the sheep would "lead," that was the direction that they would take. They would terrorize the local people day in and out. That was the environment in which my family grew up.

One day, they entered Professor Epelu-Opio's homestead and commandeered it, setting up their headquarters there. At that time, the humble professor's very own mother was staying there. Given the ruthless manner in which these rebels dealt with the people, she could no longer stay in her house. She had to move elsewhere. That was how the professor lost his house and everything he owned in the village. In the meantime, he was still working as the head of department at the College of Veterinary Medicine at Makerere University.

One day, in September 1990, the humble professor was summoned to State House Entebbe by the president of the Republic of Uganda, His Excellency Yoweri Kaguta Museveni. When he got there, the president informed him that he had formed a commission to look into the issues of the insurgency and bring it to an end. At the same time, a certain Sister Susan started teaching at Kangole Boys School in Karamoja. These are two totally separate and independent events, at least in the eyes of a casual observer, but not in the eyes of God Almighty. He was a master chess player over my life, making two separate and seemingly unrelated moves on the board of my life even unbeknownst to me at that time.

The president informed Professor Epelu-Opio that he had been appointed as the chairman to lead the commission. This was very sudden and unexpected. The professor was humbled by such a gesture from the head of state and immediately set out to work. His signature was to be as humble and as lowly as he could be, preferring not to overdress in suits. He also sought to be on the ground personally, holding talks from one community and clan to another, as well as holding talks with some of the leaders of the insurgents.

The fact that he came from the subregion and spoke the local dialect was a pretty wise choice by the president. You cannot underestimate the impact of the insecurity and waywardness that characterized the insurgency. One day, a train was moving from Kampala through the Teso area and was shot at. A woman traveling in the train with her child was hit by a stray bullet, and she died instantly. The news of her death spread like wildfire in the country through the national broadcaster. Unbeknownst to Professor Epelu-Opio, the victim was the wife of his colleague at the university. The heavy burden of breaking the news fell on the professor, who met his colleague at the university grounds but did not know what to say. After engaging in small talk as they walked around, the professor finally delivered the terrible news to his friend.

With the insecurity in the region, the burden was now to fetch the body and hold a proper burial. With lots of encouragement from the professor, they hired a pickup truck from a friend and made the trip safely. From that moment on, public transport was affected. The train ceased operations in that region, as well as buses. The professor was juggling between his work as the chairman of the commission and head of department at the College of Veterinary Medicine. With his exemplary work, the issue of the Teso Insurgency was resolved in less than two years! The rebel commander fled the country to Kenya.

The rest of the time the commission concentrated on matters to do with resettling the internally displaced people, reconciliation, and economic empowerment of the region. Professor Epelu-Opio literally preached peace, and the fact that he had also lost his home in the insurgency made it easy for the people to identify with him. He decided not to focus his energies on revenge. He preached forgiveness all through the region, and the message was received well.

In September 1993, while still working as the chairman of the commission, the humble professor from nowhere was appointed the deputy vice-chancellor of Makerere University. He acknowledges that he thought there were better and more senior professors at that time that could have filled up the post before him. The professor attributes all this to God, and indeed I may add that the invisible hand of the Divine was at work, preparing a way for me even before I could get there.

I can tell you, it is only God who knows the end from the beginning and vice versa. It is only him that has every detail mapped out and has a literal bird's eye view of our lives. The counsel of God is beyond my understanding. Something that seems so remotely involved or connected may be taken for granted. At times, we want to give God the credit only when we can directly link a miracle to him. My learning over the years is that the greatest miracles of God are unheralded, and they do occur in the indirect linkages of life.

There was some form of colonial work culture at the university when Professor Epelu-Opio became the deputy vice-chancellor. Immediately, he set out to change that situation, especially in his office, forming an open-door policy to anyone who needed to see him. Of course, he had all the excuses to be secluded because of the ever-increasing demand on his time. His day started very early each day for he had to be at the office by 7:00 a.m. The first task on his agenda was to clear his desk and attend to all the pending matters. Thereafter, he had instructed his secretaries that as long as he had time, anybody who wanted to see him could be allowed. From around 10:00 a.m., the deputy vice-chancellor would be engaged in several meetings of all manners within and outside the institution, including several traveling engagements. At five o'clock in the evening, the professor would be back at his desk to clear any backlog so that the necessary files would go to where they needed to be the following day. Later on, he would join his friends and colleagues at the prestigious Kampala Club, where he would unwind before heading back to his home.

After six months of being appointed deputy vice-chancellor, Professor Epelu-Opio's tenure as the chairman of the commission came to an end, and someone else took up the mantle. Now he had to concentrate fully on his work as the university don. Professor Epelu-Opio's office became very receptive to students, something that was unprecedented. He told his secretaries that the office was not his and that he did not own it. He resolved that he would use his time at that office to dispense his duties to the best of his abilities.

Indeed, as Professor Epelu-Opio looks back, he is proud to say that he has no dirt in his career. He loves being straight and honest, and he loves being a finisher. One thing that struck him, however, was the plight of the girl-child, especially from the Teso Subregion. He always wanted to do something about it, and in the ensuing years, as word about his benevolence went round, myriads of students passed through his office for consultation, mentoring, and encouragement.

This was not necessarily in his job description as the deputy vice-chancellor; it was something that came from his heart as a human being. He says that that is how God created him—he gave him a heart that seeks the best for other people, and as much as it is in his power, he will not shy away from helping people.

Tracing back the professor's life, one may tend to think that all his progression was random or, as we put it, "organic." I tend to think that he was at the right place at the right time doing the right thing because of a divine appointment!

Chapter 18

Missed Sponsorship? No Problem!

The sun was up and hot over Karamoja early in the morning. I had great responsibilities that day. The library had to be managed, and I had to finish assessing my senior 1 students' work. This was a new and exciting frontier for me.

As the days came to a close in Kalungu GTC, I started looking forward. I did not want to go home and languish during the senior 6 vacation. I therefore approached the Sacred Sisters, the school administration, and asked them if I could come back to Kalungu GTC and teach there or assist in any way. They found the suggestion quite good and immediately allocated me to Kangole Girls, my previous dream school! I went back to Kangole, the same school that I had appointed for myself four years before. This time around, I went as an accomplished scholar, ready to instruct the younger ones.

It was a complete metamorphosis. I really loved my students, and they did love me back. Nothing is as fulfilling in life as helping transform the life of another person through teaching. For me, the best of the students in my class were not necessarily the smart ones but the ones who showed genuine hunger to learn. They reminded me of my early days in primary school and also of my days in Kangole. I taught as if it was a calling because I knew how critical it was to empower these girls. I had come face-to-face with abject poverty, and I knew at that time that the greatest victims of abject poverty were the women and their children. I knew at Kangole as I taught my fellow girls in English that if they could be educated at least to the level that I had reached, then their communities would be transformed slowly.

The real economics of families are run by women. They are the ones in charge of the day-to-day life of the family as well as the schooling of the children. They are the ones who take care of these children. At the Makerere University student hall called Mary Stuart, there is an aging signpost in front of the hall that reads, *"Train a woman, a nation is trained!"* Oh how succinct that word is! If somebody had trained my mom, chances are that I would never have gone through the hardships that I went through as a child. Chances are that most of my brothers and sisters, if not all, would have gotten an education. If a woman is educated, the children will be educated. If the children are educated, then the community will be educated, and life will start improving.

The case of the girl-child education is special. In my country, Uganda, at the time I am writing this, not even seventy years have passed since the very first woman set foot in a school! The progress has been slow and painful, but there are many gains that have come over the years. I know that education is not necessarily the silver bullet against poverty, but it is one of the most potent forces against this scourge. When I looked at those girls behind those desks, I did not just see numbers, I saw families. I had walked where they were now walking, stood where they were now standing, and actually felt what they were now feeling. I loved them from the bottom of my heart. And as I looked at those girls and taught them with passion, I realized that I had not achieved what I had set to do. I had only completed my senior 6–level examinations. Indeed, I had come a very long way. I only had one more push to give in order to get to the very top of my endeavor in education.

The results were almost getting out, and I was beginning to feel jittery. I would be the very first female in my clan to attend university ever since God created Adam! What a feat! Sister Susan and I were banking heavily on government sponsorship. The government of Uganda must, by all means, be lauded for the fact that in every single year, the government sponsors students across the country who qualify for government sponsorship. The government pays all their tuition, accommodation, and upkeep for a period of three years to five years, depending on the course, until the students are through with their studies.

I do not have words good enough to thank the government of Uganda for this initiative. The government selects these students each year based on preset selection criteria. The students are then admitted to Makerere University, one of the leading universities in Africa, whose alumni include former presidents of the Republics of Kenya and Tanzania. For a child who has had a challenging background like I had in my life to finally get someone to pay all the necessary expenses for their higher education, it is something that no words can express how much I thank you. When you have educated a child, you have given them life. You have given them the necessary tools to face the ever-changing, fast-paced world. You have given them a ticket and permission to be people of worth and significance.

The school administration at Kalungu GTC, my "mother," Sister Susan, and I were well aware that I would get the government sponsorship. It was a given. I was excited about it. When the results did finally come, I did not have to travel to Kalungu GTC to know my fate. Kangole Girls was affiliated to Kalungu GTC for they were under the same Society of the Sacred Heart Sisters organization. The teachers were very excited about my results when they came out. I had fifteen points, scoring the famous "BBC." I got grade B in history, B in economics, and C in divinity. Fifteen points were well within the margin of getting a government sponsorship for that was the criteria that the government had used the previous year. The pretty-much-coveted government sponsorship was well within my grasp.

When the results were out, the Sisters at Kangole traveled to Kampala, the capital city of Uganda. They went there to check those of us who were fortunate to get onto the government-sponsorship scheme. We all waited with baited breath.

When they did come back, I could not handle the suspense, but I could also see in their faces that something was off. They reported that I was not on that list. You know, when you watch movies, there comes a moment when they use the slow motion to emphasize a transition or a critical aspect of the story line. From the moment I was told that my name was not on the government-sponsorship list, everything else in my life became blurry. Where was I going to get the finances to cater to my tuition at the university? How in the world had I missed that opportunity? There must have been an error. Probably those who went to check the results were not careful enough. Maybe they were in a hurry to check.

For a period of over one week, I operated on "autopilot," where my mind shuts off to protect me from harm. I cannot remember any single activity I did during that week. One thing I do remember, though, is that I could not get sleep at all! I could not function. I was slowly breaking down. You see, that was what education was to me. Its importance had been deeply ingrained in my psyche that I could not imagine not getting this chance. I thought that I was one of the most deserving students to receive it. Why did life go on a witch hunt and never give me a break? That was so unfair! I quickly resolved to go to Kampala and do the checking myself. When I got there, I confirmed my fears. That year, the government was taking "sponsees" who had sixteen points and above.

So I had gone through every imaginable trouble (according to me) all that while just to miss a government sponsorship by one point? One point! It reminds me of a talk I heard by Brian Tracy, who said that when a horse wins a race by a nose, it is awarded ten million dollars more than the horse that came in second. It does not mean that the first horse was ten million times faster than the second. No, it just won the race by a *nose*! And by the same token, my life was hanging in the balance once again, but this time around by just one point! One point was standing between me and a university education—the power of one. Without one, one cannot be a millionaire. I am even told that one day, the difference that catapulted

Hitler to be the leader of his party was one vote! And now one point was my nightmare. Hadn't I done enough? Wasn't I deserving?

The first thing that we are given in life when we are born is options. We grow all the way to adults by exploiting options. In fact, the very first thing that poverty takes away from people is the comfort of having options. Jesus Christ talked about the narrow path and the broad path—options. Moses talked about blessings and curses—options. For me, going to school was no longer an option. The option was in *how* I will pay for the university.

At this point in time, you need to realize that studying at the university is much more expensive than studying in high school. One needs to pay for tuition, accommodation, examination fees, and food. My option, as usual, was faith. At that point also, I had the luxury of leaning on Sister Susan, who was effectively like my mom, for moral support. That is another great thing that can move mountains more than money can.

After conferring with her, she encouraged me to apply for private sponsorship at Makerere University. That meant that I would be given a chance to study at this prestigious institution at my own expense. I had no idea where the money would be coming from, but I could not be stuck with this fact at all. That was my forte! That was my territory. I had been in situations where I did not know where the money would come from countless times, and each time I had pulled through. It is just that that situation was not a walk in the park.

Walking by faith, especially when you are not a true believer, is not a joke. However, I can tell you that very many people in poverty-stricken countries do walk by faith each day of their lives. They see miracles upon miracles countless times, like a child frolicking around years later after falling sick in the middle of the night when the family does not have medicine. In fact, if you ask some people how they pulled it off, how they made it through the hardships, they will tell you a simple, three-worded sentence, "I don't know." And it is true.

There are families whose members have serious sickness such as kidney failure that requires thousands of dollars each week for dialysis. And these are poor families. Each week, they scrape by and pay for a session or two of dialysis. For months on end, they live by faith. If you ask them how they made it in two or three years, they cannot really tell you how.

For me, walking by faith was then becoming a mainstay, never mind that I did not even know what faith meant, but I exercised it. I had to travel to Kampala in order to make the necessary arrangements and applications. At that time, as I was picking the forms up and making applications, I would not have made it without accommodation in Kampala. It was not something that could be done in one day. Thankfully, my economics teacher recommended a relative of his where I could be housed as I chased the admission. I did not have a single relative, even a distant relative, in the capital city. This family stayed in Mulago, which was about two or so kilometers from Makerere University. They were born-again Christians. Their religion, however, did not have an influence on me that day.

I wanted to apply for law studies, but just as I could not do art in Kalungu GTC, law was a luxury course for me because it was expensive. But I know that had I taken law as a course, I would have managed it and would have been one of the finest lawyers around. Not only did I have the intelligence, but I had also qualified for the same. I therefore applied for social sciences, which was the second-cheapest course at the university at that time. My stay in Kampala was successful, and I got my chance to study social sciences at Makerere University.

That was the easy part. The interesting part was how I would be able to gather the tuition. Now, I was in for three good years! We are talking about the beginning of the semester, and I had nothing to raise as tuition. I had no resources for accommodation, food, and academic tools. That girl-child was typically stuck. But the dream lived on. Sister Susan was a massive encourager and also an epitome of one who walked by faith. She said, "Betty, you *deserve* university education. Make sure you make an application."

So now that I had the chance, I informed her of the development. I told her that I had nothing to help me get the admission and pay the tuition. When people are rewarded for their good deeds, Sister Susan will be among the very brightest stars in heaven. Once she knew that I had admission at the university, she started looking around for private sponsors. It was not easy. But she took it as if she was fighting for her own flesh and blood. Soon enough, there was a priest who was willing to pay for all my education, glory to God!

However, there was a condition: I had to go to National Teachers' Training College (NTTC) instead of Makerere University! What do you think we did? Of course, we took the money and used it to pay for first the semester at Makerere University! God forgive us! We lied to a priest! When the priest found out what we had done, that was the end of that source of income.

The tuition was paid, but the accommodation was lacking. When I got my admission, I was assigned to Mary Stuart Hall of residence for ladies at the university. I, however, did not have money to pay for that accommodation. The relative to my economics teacher at Kalungu GTC came in handy. I would go on foot for lectures every day. That was how the first semester was paid for. There was one more semester to go for first year.

Meanwhile, I found out that I would still have qualified on government sponsorship! You know, Jesus Christ said, *"You shall know the truth and the truth shall set you free."*[4] I did not know the truth pertaining to my admission on government scholarship. The truth was that my participation in athletics at the national level meant that I earned an extra *five points*! There I was, operating under the confines of the margin of one point, yet I had five good points out there that I earned through my gift and talent! That

---

[4]   John 8:32

meant that instead of fifteen points, I would be in with *twenty points*! There would have been no discussion about securing government sponsorship. My woe is that I did not know this information! I also did not know anybody who would have pushed it for me on that account! Apparently, it was not an automatic thing.

Anyway, once I found out, I kicked into gear trying to secure my well-deserved government sponsorship. I was told to produce my National Competitions Certificate to prove it. I did not have that certificate. I was asked to get a recommendation for the National Council of Sports. I got there and talked to the general secretary. She was a very nice woman who understood my predicament and really felt bad that I had to go through what I was going through at that moment. She had no problem jotting down the recommendation letter.

However, when I got back with the letter, I was told that the scheme had already kicked off for that year and that I could not be accepted into it. I was told that I had to wait until the second lot was selected and make my application. One wonders why they did not tell me that information at first. Probably they thought that if they complicated things for me, I would give up. They did not realize that at some point I was called Punda for donkey and my stubbornness and determination was like those of a mule! To cut the long story short, the well-deserved government sponsorship never came my way no matter how long and hard I tried. Did I cry? I cannot remember!

When the second semester came by, I had no idea where Sister Susan got the money to pay for my tuition. But I am grateful she did. Up to today, I have never understood why a stranger would go out of her way to pay school fees for a child whose relatives she does not even know. But I am grateful that she was my angel at that time.

People compose love songs about crossing oceans for others, going to the moon and the stars, and such things that make you have goose bumps. For me, that was true love—caring for a stranger and not knowing whether they would ever repay you for your kindness.

Once again, may God himself look down upon my angel, my second mother, Sister Susan. If there was no Sister Susan in my life, chances are that you would not be reading my story.

Chapter 19

No Accommodation? No Problem!

Like I mentioned earlier, tuition was not the only thing that I would worry about. I also had to worry about my accommodation. The people I stayed with did not have a big house. It was a two-roomed house. One room was like the bedroom, and the other room was a sitting room. There were also very many people that depended on them, so I started feeling like I was an unnecessary burden to them. During that time, I was running around like a headless chicken trying to make ends meet so I could pay my school fees and accommodation.

I found out that there was a needy-students scheme at the university where you could apply and work as a casual in some departments. They would then pay you at the end of each month. I immediately applied. Thank God I got accepted. The cash that I would get out of it was not enough to pay for my accommodation at Mary Stuart Hall anyway. I still felt so uneasy burdening the relative of my former economics teacher at Kalungu GTC by staying at their house. I wanted to find a place where I could get good accommodation.

As fate would have it, a fellow sports lady at the campus introduced to me a grand idea. In our high school days, we had met several times at the national sports competitions. This lady hailed from Kotido. However, as she was clearing her higher education at Makerere University, I was just joining. She was attached to Mary Stuart Hall and had a room in there. In my predicaments of finding accommodation, I ended up sharing a bed with her for the better part of the first semester before she completed and had to leave. She knew about my situation to the uttermost, and as she was leaving, she was the one who suggested another great idea for my accommodation where I would not have to pay anything! I was excited!

At the university grounds, there was a sports pavilion that was basically the changing rooms. It had long benches inside and doors. During those days, very many murders were committed at the vicinity of the sports ground. However, as I was robbed of options, the university sports pavilion became my "hostel." I arranged the benches properly and placed my mattress there. My friend took me there just before she left the university. That was where I spent my second semester in my first year at Makerere University. The good news, however, was that I did not have to pay anybody for that accommodation. For a season of time, the accommodation conundrum that I faced was sorted out, thanks to my daring spirit and my ingenuity. They say, "Necessity is the mother of invention." For me, at that time, it was not just a necessity to have an education. The die had been cast a long time ago in my deepest spirit that I would have an education no matter what. It wasn't a necessity; it was my life! So I am sorry, but I have no apologies when I corrupt that saying by declaring, "Life aspirations are the mother of invention. I do not know what was going on in my head at that time, but I couldn't really care less. I had an accommodation. I was no longer feeling like a burden to anyone. It was much closer to the lecture halls. I did not have to commute.

There were certainly many advantages for someone—a girl, for that matter—staying at the changing rooms each night. The disadvantage was the risk of anything happening to me at any time. There was arguably no protection for me at all. I was on my own. The other disadvantages were the sanitation of the place, the mosquitoes at night, and the cold seasons. But what is a mosquito as compared to a Karamojong warrior? What is a mosquito bite as compared to the beatings inflicted on me by my uncle's wife? What is this danger as compared to the time that I had been left all alone in Amudat to fend for myself as a young teenager? I do not know if I was scared at that time.

Of course, the news did spread that I had converted that place into my hostel. Chances are that as the "true rumors" spread in campus, it would have attracted any riffraff who would have wanted to take advantage of me and do me bodily harm. But I stayed there anyway. One day, in another life, I may meet some real angels who are on guard, watching over me. I am convinced of that. Well, instead of the news spreading to the wrong people, it actually did spread to the right ones! And for me, the right people did not need to hear that story because they would take action against me.

Naturally, that bliss did not last for a long while. What do you think? Word got to the dean of students that I was sleeping at the sports pavilion. This did not go down well with him at all! He summoned me to his office with such urgency that I knew that my peaceful days were over even before I met him. I knew as I made my way to his office that once again, I would have to dig deep into my faith reserves to sort out my situation. In the process of time, my academic performance at campus was at an all-time low. I was emaciated and looked ghostly. I think wind would have blown me away by aiming a fan at me.

This was my umpteenth year since I first encountered trouble. Trouble and I knew each other intimately. I had grown so attached to the sports pavilion, but at the back of my mind, I had learned that for me, good things normally did not last long. At least that was the pattern of my life year in and out. My life was a typical Forex trade graph filled with troughs and bumps all through. Whether it was going up, the troughs were there. Whether it was going down, the bumps were there too.

As I stepped into the dean's office, there was absolutely nothing on me or about me that would have made the day go well for me. The dean was stern with me. He knew that it was irresponsible of me to sleep at the pavilion, a few meters from where students were being murdered occasionally. It was basically like committing suicide. He ordered me out of the pavilion with immediate effect!

And as life had always done for me, there was no option provided. That was worse than the first time I was admitted at Makerere. I could not go back to Mulago, at my economics teacher's relative. I had exiled myself, and besides, they were not expecting me! Even if they did expect me, they did not have enough resources and amenities to cater to me. I had absolutely no relative or trusted friend at the university who could help me. My earnings as a casual were so meager, only catering for my food. But a girl has got to learn. That was an already-settled deal in my heart years back.

Chapter 20

Enter the Moment, Enter the Man!

Friends, sometimes when you have come to the end of your rope, life looks at you and gives you another chance. In fact, at those moments when you are feeling like you are being buried, you may not know that you actually are being planted. This happened to me when I had been taken to Arengesiep. When I came back to Amudat (not having the means to travel back and having to do that all alone for the very first time), I found my Uncle Nicholas gone. I thought I was being buried, but actually, I was planted. That was when I got my opportunity to go to Kangole Girls. At the school, when I was bitten by a snake and nobody came to visit me, having a hospital bill to contend with, I thought I was being buried. But it was through that that I met my angel, Sister Susan. I can tell you that this happens over and over again to countless millions of people all over the world.

So as the dean ordered me out of my blessed sports pavilion, I thought that the very worst was happening to me. During that time, someone mentioned to me that we, at campus, had a very good deputy vice-chancellor by the name of Professor Epelu-Opio. They told me that I should seek his audience and tell him about my predicaments. Probably, he could provide options for me.

I had grown up to be a girl who did not shy away from options. When I realized that I could sell waragi in Kenya, I took up the opportunity and spoke to an elderly lady, convincing her to take me with her. So I had run an export business, if you will. When a friend of mine wanted me to work at the cotton plantation in Serere, I had to convince the supervisor. I took up that opportunity. When there was a chance to go to Ngora High, I took up the opportunity without second-guessing. I had already done the same with Kangole Girls and was successful. I tell you, a girl has to study!

So when this opportunity presented itself, what do you think I did? Immediately, I was knocking at the professor's office. Professor Epelu-Opio had two secretaries working for him then. They asked me what my situation was and why I needed to see the professor. I was honest with them. This was a totally different case unlike when I was seeking for admission at Kangole Girls for the first time. In this case, I just had to state my predicament.

I told them that I was an orphan and that I did not have anyone to take care of me in Kampala. I told them that I had struggled to pay tuition and did not have enough money for accommodation and food. I told them the truth about my sleeping at the dangerous sports pavilion for the better part of that semester. I informed them of how the dean of students had kicked me out of the pavilion and now I did not have anywhere to stay. I narrated to them the circumstances under which I missed the government sponsorship and that I was waiting for the next intake in the new year to know my fate. I had to study in the meantime, and I was desperately stuck.

Friends, I am sure that these ladies had heard all manner of stories from students across the whole country who were going through this and that. I am aware that people in such positions can easily get so familiar with the misery that they hear that it no longer touches their hearts. There are cases of nurses in some government hospitals who see death daily that they really have grown tough skins or hearts; nothing they see or hear touches them anymore. That was not the case with these two ladies.

They were gracious and compassionate with me. They were moved by my story. They booked for me an appointment with Professor Epelu-Opio and instructed me to make sure that I get to the office as early as 7:00 a.m. the following day. Of course, that was not a problem for me at all. Early the following morning, before Professor Epelu-Opio could get in the office, I was seated, waiting patiently for him. The professor struck me as a very reflective, brilliant, and humane individual. He invited me to his office and asked me to tell him how he could be of help to me.

I narrated my story once again to him. After I was through, I looked up to him with baited breath, waiting for my fate. A brief moment must have passed as the professor processed my story. To me, it seemed like eternity. My heart raced so much that you could hear it beating in the room. The fact that a deputy vice-chancellor could take the time to sit down and listen to a personal problem of a girl-child was absolutely phenomenal. That was what struck me that day. The very fact that I even had an audience with him was to me an "open miracle." It provided to me hope for the next day as I pondered on my options. If that chance had not been created for me by divine providence, I do not know what I would have done. Probably, my determination to get an education would have been broken by hardship that day. But in the nick of time, indeed, in the fullness of time, Professor Epelu-Opio, another perfect stranger in my life, was presented to me.

When he finally did speak, he uttered one of the most life-defining words a vulnerable girl-child who was yearning for an education could ever hear. This stranger, whom I had just met barely twenty minutes prior, offered to pay *all* my tuition fees from that moment on all the way till I was through with my university education! Isn't that amazing? Of course, I had to fend for myself as far as accommodation, registration, and examination fees were concerned, but the biggest mountain had been moved by persistence, faith, and meeting a compassionate visionary.

I came to learn later on that the professor's act was not isolated; he has helped very many kids like me over the years. So look at me for a minute: a vulnerable girl-child, an orphan, destitute and out of options, having all her tuition fees for the rest of her stay at the university paid in full! You may want to call that luck, but it was not. Someone said that luck is when opportunity meets preparedness. Even then, you cannot say that I was prepared, that that blessing was as a result of my preparedness. That was, in all views and angles, a pure miracle. I could not have seen it as a six-year-old in Amudat, nor could I have seen it as I faced the dean of students just the previous day. As I left the dean's office, I knew that I had been buried, but actually, that was nature or the Divine's way of planting me. Now, I was ready to bloom!

As if that was not enough, as I was leaving the professor's office, he recommended me for a job at the university. He even wanted me to get accommodation at Mary Stuart Hall and made some arrangements for it to happen. However, the hall was full, and there was no space for me. That was a small hitch.

One of the professor's office secretaries took it upon herself to help sort out my accommodation problem. She contacted her brother, who owned some hostels in the vicinity. I was briefly relocated to that hostel for the remainder of the semester. They did not charge me anything! Problem solved. Professor Epelu-Opio confessed that from that moment on, my academic prowess came into full bloom.

My participation in athletics put the university on the map on several occasions. In fact, I qualified to represent Makerere University at very many World University Games events in Sydney, Australia, and Beijing China. I was the queen of short races at the university. However, due to issues in the sports administration at the university at that time, I never got to board a plane to represent my university. Besides, my studies were central to everything I did, so it did not hurt me in any way.

At the time that the World University Games were taking place, we would be having exams at campus. There was no special treatment for those who would go and participate. If you did not sit for your examinations, you would have to forego that year. It was a luxury that I would not afford. As much as I really wanted to board an airplane, I knew that if I missed one year, I would not get any more time.

So I decided to forego all those chances. At the moment when we were not having the examinations, such as the chance to go to Australia, the sports administration's corruption and recklessness could rob us of the opportunity. Later on, the person in charge was fired. There was a time when there was an opportunity for us to go, albeit during examination time. Only one girl was chosen to go by the corrupt sports regime. I did not mind because I had to sit for my examinations. However, as she traveled for the first time in her life in an airplane, she did forego her examinations. She came back with jet lag, was disoriented, and eventually dropped out of law school. Such is the cost of choosing an adventure over an education. I did not want to fall into that trap. Yes, I was gifted and talented. Yes, there could have been opportunities out there, but they were a pure gamble as compared to the academic opportunity that I had been given by the auspices of Professor Epelu-Opio and Sister Susan Anyango.

I remember there was a sports coach from Indiana State University who had a scholarship for me from that university. If you want to talk about a gamble, this was it. I had to make a decision between going to Indiana or staying at Makerere. My staying and studying at Makerere was already assured. When I inquired further from this coach about the prospects of my academic pursuits, the answers were not immediately apparent. It seemed to me like the scholarship was purely a sports scholarship. This meant that if anything happened to me physically, that scholarship would no longer hold water. I was made aware of some cases of people who did actually take such scholarships. There were some who, when they got there and failed to impress for one reason or another, got deported. Their chances for education therefore got ruined while abroad as well as when they came back here. I did not have the luxury of choice.

I needed certainty, and that Indiana chance was not a certainty at all. I was not about to gamble my life with it. My major interest was not sports. If, for some reason, I had intellectual trouble, then of course, I could have given this scholarship a thought. But I was and still am an intelligent person, and my major interest was to make sure that I got an education. It was the only way I knew to defeat poverty and lack that had plagued my mother. So I passed on that chance.

Chapter 21

Mama

Do not forget the ever-present Sister Susan. She was an earthly angel who also got helped by the professor's action of benevolence. When the professor helped me, he lessened her burden. Now she was able to cater to my pocket money and other amenities. She could also physically bring me food at the university. God bless her over and over again. She was like my very own mother. I will forever remain her daughter, and she will forever remain my mother. There is nothing I have done in my life that Sister Susan is not aware of.

It is interesting because I was not so close to my very own flesh-and-blood mom. I only saw her twice as a child and never as an adult. When I worked in Serere, we could also meet on occasions. There was this time while I was in Serere that I will never forget. Back then, I used to run errands using a bicycle. In fact, in the whole town, I was known as one of the fastest cyclists around.

One day, as I was supposed to go back to school, I cycled all the way to where Mama was staying, quite a bit of a distance. When my time to go back came, she decided to accompany me on another bicycle. So as you can imagine, I was ahead of her in our small journey on our bikes as she tailed me. As we were just about to get to my cousin's home, something happened. The chain in Mama's bike snapped, and she lost control. She came crashing right into me and took me off-balance. We both went sprawling on the dusty roads of Serere.

Mama was shocked and became delirious. She, for a split second, imagined that she had caused an accident that had killed her daughter. She started wailing out loud, "I have killed my daughter! God help me!" I just got up unscathed, probably with a few bruises. I told her not to worry and that I was fine. That day, I had an up close encounter with what my mom felt about me. She loved me and cared for me, and she wanted the best for me. She was so fond of me. I have no doubt about it.

In short, there are countable times that I have had a real conversation with my mom. Of course, her love for me was unquestionable. I remember when she was so furious with Uncle Nicholas when I first went to visit her while in primary school. Seeing her daughter with scars suggesting massive beatings broke her heart so much. She had decided that Uncle Nicholas would not go away with me again.

However, she was not powerful enough. The clan had given Uncle Nicholas jurisdiction over my dad's family, and his word was final. He had even been given the command to marry her, something that he declined because he was still in a teachers' college at that time and because he did not want to take responsibility of seven children and their widowed mom. So he prevailed upon her to take me back to Amudat, a decision that I think was brilliant. Had I stayed in Serere with my mom, chances are that you would not be reading this book. There is no question in my spirit that Mom loved me and cared about me. That is a fact that I do know. But Mommy was seriously affected by the untimely death of her husband.

You know, you can never plan with death, especially death as cruel and sudden as that of my father. Up until then, she was a respected woman of the society who was taking care of her husband's household, the household of the local subparish chief. Of course, very many people knew her. As long as her husband was alive, he took care of everything—not just his nuclear family, but also the extended family. My dad provided for his parents, his brothers, and his sister. He was a very generous man. But how does a woman recover from the sudden loss of her husband? How does an uneducated woman juggle the burden of feeding and schooling seven children? How does she handle the life of widowhood, especially at a very young age of thirty?

I am told that Mama later on took to drinking. She had a relationship with another man in Serere who was rumored to be a powerful herbal doctor. She met him at a "landing site" at the shore of Lake Kyoga where she worked trying to provide for my brothers and sisters. As long as she was with him in Serere, she was fine. But when she could travel to Katakwi, she would develop some semblance of boils on the head. They would cause her grievous pain and suffering. She lost a lot of weight. She lost her peace and lost her direction in life. It must have been a very tough moment for my brothers and sisters who stayed with her. I imagine what Peter and Samson went through seeing their beloved mother disintegrate.

That is what poverty does to people and to families. That is why, to date, I have a phobia for poverty. I am an avowed enemy of poverty through and through. The very first and immediate victims of abject poverty are the women: the wife, the widow, and the girl-child. I cannot begin to imagine what was going through my mom's mind as she tried to eke out a living for herself and her children. Her life had been so rosy in the initial stages of courtship and marriage. But after giving birth to seven children and the subsequent death of her husband, things were never the same.

A mother always wants the best for her children. It tears her apart to know that she cannot provide for her children as she would have wished. It tears her apart to know that she is helpless and has no resources to even make her have a say in the direction of the lives that her children would have taken. Can you imagine bearing children and not living with them for over a decade? Can you imagine never hearing from that child and never seeing that child for prolonged periods? And that is the very child that you bore, the very child that you brought forth in labor, the very child that was born to you looking perfect, innocent, and in need of love, tenderness, and care. And now that child is a world apart from you, trying to fend for her own

149

life, while you are still alive and have no say and no way of chipping in and helping alleviate her hardship! It can be so traumatizing to know that you are the one who brought forth that child and you cannot help her.

That must have been the torment that my destitute mom suffered each and every waking day of her life from the time that our beloved papa passed on unexpectedly.

In the meantime, Mama did not need to worry about me. I was a happy girl. I was the only girl-child, probably the only child, to come from my village and clan who was at a university. Against all the odds that I had faced, that girl-child was now receiving the highest form of education available in the Pearl of Africa. Not only was I excelling in my classes and in the course units that I took; I was also excelling in my giftedness in athletics. I represented the university very many times in short races at very many competitions.

You could easily say that my struggles were soon becoming a thing of the past. Life was becoming easier by the day. My class attendance was assured. One tiny detail about my accommodation, though: when the grace period that I had been given at the hostel elapsed, I could not again afford to foot the accommodation bills. I did what only I could do: I went back to the sports pavilion. A lady had to study, you know. And ladies and gentlemen, that was where I spent my two years at campus each night until I was through with my final examinations. No harm befell me while I was there, something that I was very grateful for.

One day, during the second semester, I had the massive privilege to represent Makerere University in the East African Interuniversity Athletics Meeting. This meeting was taking place at Egerton University in Kenya. As usual, I performed admiringly well. However, there was something nudging my spirit benignly that could not just go away. For some reason, I just felt some somberness, disquietness, apprehension, and disturbance in my spirit. I did not know what it was, and I probably might not be able to describe it amicably well. But I knew in my heart of hearts that something was wrong. I could not put my finger on it, but my heart was involuntarily heavy. For some reason, I wanted to head back home immediately after we got back to Uganda from the Kenya trip. And that is exactly what I did. There was some heavy urgency in my spirit to get home.

When I alighted from the bus in Katakwi, I was surprised to have seen my boyfriend. He had been waiting for me all along, and for some reason, he just thought that I would be traveling back home. He had been a longtime friend from the time I was in Kangole Girls Senior Secondary School.

Our friendship was casual, but with time, it grew to a full-blown love relationship. In my heart of hearts, I knew that I would marry him one day. However, I was not stupid to engage in relationship overdrives at that moment in my life. I had to get an education first, and I let him know as much. He agreed that it was important and that he would wait for me until I finished my schooling. I was a happy girl. It was so refreshing to see him at that shopping center in Katakwi.

Immediately, as we saw each other, he told me that I had to hurry home because everything was not right. All that was just confirming that urgency that I had in my spirit that something was grossly wrong. I did not want to ask him to tell me what the problem was exactly, so I trudged along home, dreading what I would find there with each step that I took.

Ladies and gentlemen, when I got home, there was a small group of people gathered. Our home was like a deserted funeral place. It was so for one reason: my beloved mama had passed away and had been buried two days to the day I arrived home. Finally, poverty had had its last laugh after running rings around my mama. There was, laid to rest, a woman who did not know the full whereabouts of her fifth-born child. And there stood a girl who had barely known her mother. The two of us had been brutally separated by the scourge of poverty, an enemy that I had vowed to fight with all my might by getting an education. It was an enemy that had fought me every inch of the way, not wanting to give me any breathing space. It was a relentless enemy, a lying and suffocating enemy, that killed the spirit before it robbed people of life entirely. It had done a number on my mama. She was now six feet under the earth, completely outdone by poverty.

Waves upon waves of sorrow swept over me with full force. I had lost a dad while a toddler, not knowing right from wrong. I do not even remember his face, save for what I see in a photograph. I had been separated from my family in order to seek an education. I had been abandoned by my beloved Uncle Nicholas. I had suffered year in and year out while trying to get an education. I had survived all these things through sheer resilience and determination. Finally, I had a smile on my face, and life was quite normal to me. I knew that once I was through with school and everything went according to plan, I would have helped my mom out of her desperate state and given her a decent life. I would have bought her better clothes, built her a big and nice house, given her good food, and just spoiled her! But I had been time-barred.

Poverty had an overreach in our lifelong bout and had landed a mightily heavy punch. I was like a boxer who had received an uppercut unexpectedly and was now sprawling on the canvas as the referee counted me out. There was nothing I could do to help my dear mama.

Wiping my tears from my eyes, I knew that I would never be the same again after that day. I was officially an orphan, robbed of both parents. Yet all was not lost. Nature or divine providence had replaced my dad with Professor Epelu-Opio and my dear mom with Sister Susan. Indeed, I was not alone. I was covered.

From my base at the sports pavilion in Makerere University, I continued to pursue my education. Sure enough, in the fullness of time, what had started as a struggle that did not know an end indeed did come to an end. On my graduation day, Sister Susan and my brother Samson were there to witness the fruits of our labors.

The graduation party was held at a certain Mr. John Kidimu's house, Sister Susan's brother-in-law. He had come to the rescue of Sister Susan some years back in paying her school fees when her mother was struggling to make ends meet. The connection was now complete. He was hosting the fruits of the first generation of his giving heart and seeing firsthand what his benevolence decades earlier had just yielded.

Such moments are moments of great reward to the giver. One of the things that make our lives worth living is the contribution we make in order to bring possibilities in other people's lives to fruition. John Kidimu did it for Sister Susan. Had he not done so, we do not know what Sister Susan would have ended up like. That he did it for her opened the door for me to receive the blessing through her giving heart. And that was how the cycle came to full completion. At the time of his giving, he had no idea how many people he would impact. Indeed, when Sister Susan is reaping her rewards for the numerous lives she has touched positively, the benefits are also to her brother-in-law, Mr. John Kidimu.

I missed the first-class honors by a whisker and graduated with the upper second-class honors degree—the very first degree in our clan probably since Adam was created!

Part 5

Free at Last?

Chapter 22

Unexpected Motherhood!

Someone has written a very good book entitled *After University What Next?* It is a very good read. One of the interesting things in life is that you really never graduate from it. There is always a "next." You can always be better. Another person said, "Good, better, best—do not let it rest until the good is better and the better is best." The roller coaster of my childhood and education as a girl-child had effectively come to an end. The crown of it all was a great performance that I had at my examinations. As I have already shared, I only missed the first-class honors by a whisker, a matter of fractions of points. To have achieved that feat as a vulnerable girl-child, through all the mishaps and hardships that I faced, is simply incredible.

I am here today to inspire as many people as I can to hear my voice because my coach tells me that #YourVoiceChangesEverything. There are very many people who have not started because they want to see the whole staircase before they can start climbing. They want to see the finances for publishing the book before they can start writing their manuscript. They want to see all the capital needed to start their business before they can even write a business plan for it. Of course, it will be wonderful to have everything in place before you get started.

However, I have come to learn that life operates, for the most part, in bits and pieces. Life unfolds one step at a time, and the next step is only clear based on the thoroughness on your part in the previous step. That is how progress is made. Apostle Paul calls it "From glory to glory." It is a cycle that always gets better.

That is why we today are technologically better off than our forefathers in many things. Had I waited to have everything in place for my studies, I would never have made it. At times, the steps I am talking about in life can be broken down to days and, at extreme times, to hours. It is a life of faith and determination.

Had I achieved what I set out to do initially? Partially, yes. Yet the conditions of my life were not any better. In the days of my parents, someone who had upper second-class honors in any field would be assured of employment with the government and with prospects of growing. Things, of course, have changed since then. It was not that easy to get a job, and I quickly found out that in the job world, you also need connections. No, I am not talking about people who can force you into positions that you do not qualify for, but I am talking about people who will know where your options are. Such people will point you to the correct door, but what you do when going through that door will be totally up to you.

Luckily for me, I was still working as a casual at the university. So I did hang around there for a while. I did not retreat back to the village. That would have been counterproductive.

I rented a room at a place called Kalerwe, about three or four kilometers from the university. Oozing hope and determination, I brought my two younger sisters to Kampala to stay with me and started educating them. I did this with the meager salary that I got working at the university as a casual worker. I felt a sense of responsibility for them, and I wanted them to be educated like I was. I was doing this as a contribution on my part in their lives. However, they were not as gifted intellectually as I was, and so they did not continue with their studies to the level I had reached.

Professor Epelu-Opio was so proud of my academic accomplishment. He recommended me to the Faculty of Social Sciences and specifically the Gender and Women Studies Department. Somehow, it was the right move for me because I was so passionate about women and girls. Of all the people that I have ever sponsored in education, a bulk of them were women and girls.

I applied at that department to become a junior lecturer. However, my academic papers were delayed in coming out, and so the chance kept pending. So as I waited for that to be sorted out, I helped around doing this and that at the department. Some of the things that I would do were exams invigilation, preparation of tutorials, and many other things that lecturers would do. While at that department, it occurred to me that I could still further my studies, this time specifically in gender and women studies.

With my impeccable academic record, it was easy to get an admission; however, I could not raise the necessary funds needed for this higher education. You see, immediately after I was through with my university education, I wanted to fulfill the promise that I had made to my boyfriend that I would marry him. It was in my mind.

In our dating and courtship all those years, I had kept myself for him. My goal to get an education was firm, and everything else became subservient to that goal, including my relationships.

He was such a good man those days. He used to travel to Kampala to visit me, and in fact, shortly after I finished my examinations, I became expectant. In fact, by the time I was graduating, I was a few months pregnant. At some point, the prenatal period did cost me a position in the district local government. After the interviews, I could not be taken, although I was the best.

When my boyfriend started earning a salary, he became a changed man. There were some things that happened that I would not want to go into the details here. But in a nutshell, our relationship came to that point in time that we had to reevaluate. There was a very major issue on trust and faithfulness that we had to overcome. Mind you, I had developed a very negative attitude about men and marriage due to the circumstances under which I was brought up. After a few confrontations, we forgave each other and decided to keep at it.

Our friendship continued largely because of the promise I had made myself as a young girl. I had said that the first person that I would date would be the person that I would marry. For some reason, I thought it was not proper to date more than one person; I thought it was not right.

So that belief system and mind-set contributed to me extending an olive branch to the relationship. However, the change I expected in our relationship never really happened. The challenges that we had on trust and faithfulness continued reoccurring, and that really had a heavy impact on me.

Up to now, as I look back, I can tell you that there is no question in my heart that the two of us were in love. There is no question in my heart that we loved each other truly, seeing that we started out as friends at a very young age. However, as any married couple would realize, love is not the feeling that cements a relationship and sustains it. Love is simply a bonus. However, for the relationship to work, there must be hard work, mutual respect, vision, patience, and forbearance for both parties.

In the Bible, there is a major question that is asked, *"How can two walk together unless they agree?"*[5] Do you know you can be in love all you want but that if you are not in agreement concerning serious issues about your future, your values, and what matters in life, that relationship will not last the test of time?

A time came, however, when I had to stand up and make a decision about my future. I came to the realization that there would be no respite in our relationship. I noticed that the cycle that we were going through would keep repeating itself over and over again, and each time, it would leave me heartbroken and shaken to the core. Something had to give. The latest incident really massively broke my heart for it happened right under my nose.

---

[5]   Amos 3:3

I knew right then and there that that kind of a relationship would be serious trouble in my life if I continued forcing it to work. The straw that broke the camel's back was actually the same straw as the previous ones that had been piling over and over again: trust, unfaithfulness, harshness.

To me, I knew at the back of my mind that there was no way that such a situation would be remedied, especially when there was no remorse and repentance. I was happy with the fact that I was not married, and that was a big break for me as well as a perfect chance to draw a line in the sand, stake my claim on what I deserved, and move on. So move on I did. Just because I had a past with him did not guarantee a future with him.

I let him know that I could not continue the relationship with him, citing my lost trust and bringing to the fore the reasons why I felt so. We parted ways. I was blessed with a bouncing baby boy who was a joy to me. The breakup was something that shook the both of us heavily. He found it so hard to let go. He had access to my house still and would come at his own will anytime he wished. Although we had ended our relationship, we still had issues to resolve every now and then because he had not moved on from it completely.

The quality of the life and success you have is directly dependent on the type of person you choose to live with. I was determined to have a better and quality life than that which I had seen in Amudat, Serere, and Katakwi, and I knew that with that man, that would not be a reality.

So taking care of my siblings as well as my son needed lots of effort and finances that I decided to forego the opportunity to study for my master's to date.

Chapter 23

From Best Tea Girl Ever to HR Consultant

While still waiting for the employment as a junior lecturer, I was given a job at Makerere Institute of Social Research (MISR). My job title was graduate research fellow. I was so proud of myself to finally have a job title to my name. Things were getting better and better for me despite the mishaps that I faced. The plan at the job was to go to the field and collect data and take an active part in data analysis if need be.

Like I said, that was the plan. It ended up not being put into effect. For me to do the research, the organization needed to have the projects running. Without the projects, there was no "work" for us per se. However, the organization kept us ready just in case something came up so that they would not have to start recruiting and training fresh blood. In my stay there, the projects were few and far in between.

In the meanwhile, I was attached to the director's office to do clerical work. What I did was run petty errands for the director's office. In fact, I became the director's "tea girl." As much as I had a glorified title, the best I would do was to serve tea. While others would go to the field for research, I would stay at the office and run clerical errands. I do not know how that happened. I was one of the best students they had hired, and I had an upper second-class degree in social sciences! I had great potential. I think what you should do with potential is to do as much as possible to unearth it and maximize it.

Looking back as an adult, however, I realized that the head of the organization trusted me so much, and that was why she wanted to keep me around. I am sure that if we did have projects to work on, she would have had no problem letting me go to the field to join the others in research work.

I determined in my spirit that I would be the best tea girl this world had ever seen. There was no time that I went to work late. Despite the fact that I was nursing a young baby, I did not have any excuse for coming to work late. During lunch hours, my athletics would kick in as I had to run back home to breastfeed my baby. That happened all while I was at the institute. In fact, there was a day that I slipped into a manhole and sprained my leg. It was excruciatingly painful, but I did not want to tell my boss about my predicament. I did not want to look like I was a burden at work in any way.

I went about my duties with a joyful heart and did the very best that an Itesot girl could do. Each time I went back home, I was satisfied that I had given my absolute best at it. That, I believe, is the standard we should use daily in our lives. If we are not going to give something our best, then there is absolutely no point of accepting to do it in the first place. The world is full of pretenders everywhere you turn. Quality is being compromised because people hate what they have been told to do. At times, people are not being compensated well, and so their focus is not intense enough to provide quality work and products.

All in all, I would say that a spirit of excellence is a matter of choice, not something proportionate to circumstances. You decide that you will be known as a person of excellence, whether conditions are good or bad. That has been my mantra all my life, all the way from decorating my uncle's house walls in Amudat to being the best tea girl probably in the country.

In turn, I was greatly endeared to the director. She became so fond of me, and several times, she would go out of her way to give me extra cash from her own pocket. Life was not easy for me at that time since I was taking care of my baby and my sisters. I did suffer quite a bit. I am sure that had I asked for salary increment, I would have been given solely because of my spirit of excellence and not because of pity on my dire circumstances and needs. She got to know that I had a baby, and that was why she would go out of her way to chip in from her own pockets.

However, had I been a lousy employee with an attitude like I see some graduates have these days (there was one in a credible university who refused to photocopy documents because she was a graduate), I would not have been endeared to my boss. I must say I am proud of my work as a tea girl at MISR, looking back more than fourteen years ago at the time of writing this book. I settled into a routine that I followed expeditiously. Sometimes, routines protect us; but at other times, they also enslave us.

I do not know of anyone who has done the same thing over and over again for years and is still happy about it. Maybe you can say a teacher or a doctor or other career professionals. Much as they do have routines, on a daily basis, there are varieties that happen. A teacher has goals each term, and his/her joy is to see as many kids as possible graduate with honors. A good one cannot be bored with this. But for a tea girl, the only variety that she can have is probably a different-colored kettle or mug. The routine, however, is the same old rut. You can only give your best for a while, but not forever in the same thing that you might not have been born to do. There was a bit of a change at some point when I did some research work and got some good money, enough to purchase for myself a Nokia phone. Was it the first ever in my clan? I don't know.

But once again, providence came to my rescue. Professor Epelu-Opio, who by then had become like my daddy, informed me of an opening. I must insist that up to today, I still meet the professor and inform him of how my life is taking shape. At some point, he even wished that I could have been his biological child. He had become so fond of me. One thing about me is that I made a decision never to disappoint people in my life. I know I am not necessarily a people pleaser, but one rule of thumb is that when you meet people, you leave a positive mark and impression about you with them. The professor was never disappointed by the decision to fully fund my university education. So naturally, when he saw that an international organization was recruiting, he let me in on it. He might not have known anybody at that organization. All he knew was that they had employment opportunities. I attended the interview.

Ernst & Young were looking for fresh graduates who had passed very well at the university. I was on the professor's mind because of my impeccable performance, missing first-class honors by fractions of points. The professor was confident that I would make it at Ernst & Young, and he urged me to apply. He did not even know the exact details of the vacancy, but he was sure it had something to do with human resource.

In my thinking, I guessed that the vacancy was for a human resource manager. Before I got excited about it, I quickly cautioned myself in my own cheekiness by saying, "You girl, from a tea girl to a human resource manager . . ." I laughed at myself, but then I went ahead and applied. The position was for a human resource trainee consultant.

Life was not about to come to a standstill for me. I had attended an interview before and was not taken, so I was aware of that eventuality. However, there was a tinge of excitement in my spirit. When you know that your life *can* change for the better, you tend to become nervous and hyperactive. When I got to the interview room, I did not know what to expect. That was an internationally reputed organization.

I did as best as I could at the interview, but I assure you, it was a tough one. One thing about me is that I have a very jolly spirit. All the way back from childhood to Kangole, they knew me as a cheeky child. That cheekiness showed up at the interview. I also exuded an aura of being carefree. Looking back, I still remember two people in the interviewing panel. One of them went on to become the human resource and administration director at one of the most reputable government parastatals in Uganda as of the writing of this book.

After the interview, life went on as normal. I kept giving my best as the tea girl. I also informed Sister Susan about my attending the interview, and she was excited for me. I am so sure she went and prayed for me as she always does. One day, the phone rang, and it was Ernst & Young calling. Ladies and gentlemen, there comes a time in your life when a single phone call or e-mail or SMS or meeting can totally change your life forever. For me, it was that phone call. I was asked to go to their Uganda office in Kampala to pick up my appointment letter!

I had been selected, but do not fool yourself. This selection was just a trial for me. There was no strong vote of confidence for me. My fellow trainees who had been selected were already working in other consultancy firms. I was the greenest of them all. I was as raw as I could get it. My appearance did not go well at the interview. Have you ever seen a breastfeeding mother with long hair and no makeup of any kind? That was me. At times, interviewers do not know what they may be keeping away by just judging by appearance.

If you have ever watched the movie *The Pursuit of Happyness*, you will know exactly what I am talking about. I can easily identify myself with that character in the movie in quite a few ways. After the hassles he had gone through—taking care of his boy, being thrown out of his house, sleeping in public toilets with his only boy—when he knew that he had been given the job, tears blinded his eyes. For him, he knew that there would be no more days of sleeping in shelters and even missing such opportunities at times. He knew that his child would lead a comfortable life. The sun had finally shone upon him as it had done for me.

When I opened my appointment letter, you should have seen my biggest surprise. Do not hold your breath, for it was a beautiful surprise. That tea girl with an upper second-class degree in social sciences was earning a little less than 100,000 Ugandan shillings at that time. Yet this letter was telling me that I would be earning 500 percent higher than that salary! It was the most marvelous news I had ever received since Professor Epelu-Opio decided to pay for my school fees. My life would never be the same again!

That, right there, was what it was all about. Five hundred and fifty thousand shillings in a month was a figure that would take approximately two years for my mom to make doing her manual work daily.

There is a scripture that says, *"Death, where is your sting?"* And I could easily echo with it at that time and ask, *"Poverty, where is your power?"* I had fought against this scourge over my life, and I had crossed the line. I would never be the same again. My mind went on autopilot. I have no idea how I got back home, but as I walked out of that office with my appointment letter in hand, chances are that I could have been knocked down by a vehicle. I was not in my conscious mind at all. I remember going back to MISR that day and simply telling the secretary that I found there that I was off to take another job.

I did not even bother to resign; such was the extent of my excitement. My boss had traveled and was not in the office that day. I am made to understand later on that when she was told that I quit my job and left, she was disappointed that I had left! You see, that was the fruit of giving more than 100 percent of myself in the assignment I had been given.

Chapter 24

Poverty, You Are Fired!

I quickly settled down at Ernst & Young. They wanted me to get started immediately, and so I did not have the luxury of time to resign and explain things at MISR. I moved on. Although as an HR professional, I would not advise people to do that. I was a very fast learner. I gave my all to Ernst & Young, working as if my entire life, everything I had ever gone through was to take me to where I was at that moment. I worked as if my life depended on that job, and indeed it really did. Our work was an immediate consultancy with one of the government parastatals in Uganda that was undergoing restructuring at that time. I learned everything that I needed to learn, and the seeds of human resource management were planted in my life, never to be uprooted again to date.

My life also changed. I moved from a small house to a much bigger and better one. My child was now well provided for, and I was a happy mother. No longer would I need to walk or run from home to work. I had amicable resources for daily transportation.

Back at work, after a period of six months on the consulting assignment, I was adjudged to be the best of the batch that Ernst & Young had recruited. They called me the star performer of the project we worked on. As a matter of fact, I was promoted two grades ahead to grade 4. The flipside of being a fast learner is that you get bored very quickly. I came into the organization very green, not knowing anything in matters of human resource (HR). In fact, the only thing I did know about HR was a course unit I did back at Makerere. However, I had performed so well, and there was nothing particularly new for me at that place.

Naturally, I got bored. I was tired of doing job analyses, writing proposals, and writing technical and financial reports among other tasks. I wanted to be an implementer of policies, not one who wrote about them and their reports. The HR bug had bitten me, and I wanted to grow in it as a career to the very top. I wanted to pursue a master's degree in HR, banking on Ernst & Young to support me in that endeavor.

However, the policy of the company at that time was to sponsor their employees in taking ACCA courses. For me, once I fell in love with HR, there was no looking back. I knew that if I took the ACCA course, I would not be building my HR muscle that I was so desperate to. So I started feeling like the longer I stayed at Ernst & Young, the more my chances of growing in HR were limited. I did not want to continue being a consultant. A consultant in HR was totally different from an HR officer or practitioner. I wanted to diversify my practical knowledge in HR.

At that time, I was a team leader of consultants that were conducting a research on the employer-of-the-year survey in the country. There would be a competition, and the best organization was going to be awarded a prize. The best practices of the employer of the year would be shared with the rest of the survey-participating organizations in the country. It was an exciting project. It was at that time that I found out that Total Uganda was touted by one of my teams as the best implementer of the best HR policies in the country. The way they spoke so passionately about this organization made me take immediate note.

This coincided, incidentally, with my desire for more exposure in the HR industry. Secretly in my heart, I started desiring to work in such an organization as Total Uganda. Indeed, my desire became to work at Total Uganda itself so I could experience firsthand implementation of the good HR policies.

They normally say, *"When the student is ready, the teacher appears."* I got to learn through our HR circles that Total Uganda was looking for an HR officer. My investigations showed that that position came with a car. Not only did I make an application, but I also paid for my driving school lessons. In due time, I got my driver's license. I was eventually invited for the interview, which was not just one interview but a series of them. Through their consultant, I did personality profile tests and the human job analysis test before I was forwarded to meet the Total Uganda management.

In the long run, I was successful and was awarded the job! *This is what it is all about*, I thought. I was now on the ascendancy in life. But just before that, I could not dump Ernst & Young with the same enthusiasm and ease like I did MISR. When the partners learned of my being poised to move to Total Uganda, they sat me down for over two hours, trying to convince me to rescind my resignation. They thought that I had a very big future at the company.

This was a catch-22 for me for the very first time in my life. I had been used to trouble all the way, but now, I had to make a decision between better and best—such a luxury, I might add. In such negotiations, one makes you know how valuable you are. They informed me that I had been the one who was holding the forte of HR consulting in the company and that I was a crucial cog in the wheels of the organization in that area. In short, they did not see an immediately available person of my ilk who could carry on what I had been doing.

I was flattered. They told me that if I maintained course, chances were that I would be an HR partner in the company in less than five years. Leaving the company would not be a good decision. Their talk made my decision a very difficult one.

At the end of the day, I decided to leave for Total Uganda. My main consideration was the implementation of HR policies and seeing them work, other than staying in consulting. I needed a stable working environment in an organization. I figured out that my chances for growth were much more pronounced at Total Uganda than at Ernst & Young. The decision put lots of pressure on me since Total Uganda wanted me to get started immediately. I had to pay Ernst & Young equivalent of my one-month salary because of leaving at short notice. But as I left, looking forward to a great future, I knew in the deepest recesses of my heart that I had made a good decision, one that I would never have to regret.

Chapter 25

Defying Death

I am meant to understand that I was born under very spiritually curious circumstances. Word had it that while Mommy was expecting me, she was always tormented by evil spirits. This information came straight from her, and so I will just relay it to you as she told it. Our house was grass thatched. Part of her responsibilities as a woman was to repair the grass thatch from time to time.

One day, she said, as she was on the roof repairing it, evil spirits attacked her and threw her violently onto the ground. Everyone who saw the spectacle expected a fatality or, at least, a miscarriage, but they waited in vain. It did not happen. I must have refused to die at that time. She lay unconscious for a while and recovered later. People were astounded when this transpired, and I am sure some of them took note. Life, of course, went on as usual as my parents expected their fifth born anytime.

My dad, Mr. Samson Icaarat, was at that time a subparish chief in an impoverished village of Omukuny, Ongongoja Subcounty, Katakwi District, in Northeastern Uganda. Mommy said that at the time of my birth, she was all alone at home while everybody else had gone to the farm to cultivate. Like a thief in the middle of the night, the labor pains came upon her all of a sudden. With great determination, she brought me forth safely, but she was alone. Nobody helped her.

However, the placenta delayed in coming out, a situation that made her faint, leaving me lying on the ground. Were it not for an elderly relative who was passing by, I do not know what would have happened to the both of us. This relative was called Ogiel. I was named after her.

I am not interested in being super spiritual and reading so much into my past and attributing things to the spirit world. But it is clear that from the onset, even before I was born, I was up against a battle for my life. I had had a brush with death even before I was born, and I escaped with my life in different occasions as death tried to pursue and end my life.

For some reason, I just refused to die. I defied it. What was left then was a life of abject poverty, misery, suffering, and hardship. That too was something I refused to bow down to. I fought it with all the gadgets that I had. I cried, I brewed, I smuggled, I served, I dug, I pumped water, I slept in a pavilion for years, and I did many other things in direct defiance to poverty and misery. With the Total Uganda job sealed, signed, and delivered, one could say that I had won the war, but the battle was still raging. Death, however, did not give up on me. It kept tracking me in my endeavors.

If I thought that Ernst & Young had changed my life, I had not met Total yet! That position came with even higher and better perks than the ones I was getting at Ernst & Young. Total Uganda enabled its employees to purchase vehicles that they would use for work and own them once they finished paying the car loan. The organization worked with banks by guaranteeing payment of the car. The employee then had to pay bits and pieces of the loan until it was cleared. Our part was just to go to the showroom or the car bond and select the car we wanted, provided it met the safety and security specifications of the organization.

The safety and security manager would oversee this part and approve, and immediately a new employee would own a car to help him or her work better. My position included quite an amount of travel, and I was grateful that I was able to get this car. After my induction, I set off to work with the same zeal and spirit that I had had over the years. I must admit that the challenge at Total Uganda was greater than that at Ernst & Young, but it was a definite upgrade on Ernst & Young. It gave me a totally new perspective in HR, and I was enjoying what I was doing as an HR officer. I had the opportunity for the very first time to do administration work in HR, one thing that I longed to do but missed at Ernst & Young.

With time, a new managing director came in at Total Uganda. There are people in life who are great at bringing out the best from other people, and this new boss was one of them. He saw something in me that I did not see in myself. They say that you cannot see yourself when you are in the picture frame, and that is true. He saw a lot and great potential in me as an HR person, and he immediately pointed it out over and over again. After a period of six months, I was confirmed as a human resource officer at Total Uganda.

Chapter 26

"Betty, We Will Wait for You"

Part of my work included organizing regional meetings for the up-country staff. I had to do travel circuits each quarter around the country. We had fuel depots and staff in the following towns: Kampala, Entebbe, Jinja, and Mbale. There came a time, one year and approximately five months down the line after I had been confirmed as an HR personnel at Total Uganda, that my brothers decided to give our parents a proper burial. We were to have funeral rights for them.

You see, due to the Teso Insurgency and the Karamojong raids, my father was not buried at his ancestral home. It seemed to my brothers that we would appease his spirit if we organized proper rights for him. The exercise would involve exhuming his remains and transporting them to our ancestral home in Omukuny Village from Katakwi Township, where he was born. His burial was done near the township previously. When my brothers asked me about it, I did not object, much as I did not believe in doing these rites in the first place. I chose to support them, but I made them aware that I would not be available for all the days that the ceremonies were taking place. However, I had to give them a weekend that I would be available so that they would proceed to do the rights then.

I organized my itinerary to coincide with this event. On a particular Friday in October 2006, I traveled to Jinja and held the staff meeting at the Jinja depot. My intention was to do the same for the Mbale depot and then proceed home to Omukuny, Katakwi, to witness the final rites at the ceremonies. I followed my itinerary as planned. After a two-hour meeting with the staff in Jinja, about eighty kilometers from Kampala, I proceeded to Mbale to do the same. I drove for over 140 kilometers and held the two-hour meeting as required before covering over 150 kilometers to Katakwi. I arrived at around 10:00 p.m. on Friday night. On Saturday, I was fully booked, running errands the whole day and driving here and there to get this and that, because we had a funeral service the following day on Sunday. That had been organized by my brother Samson, who was still a catechist at his Catholic church.

The company policy did not allow me to give the vehicle to anyone to drive. That day, I was the only person who had a car, save for the priests who had traveled quite a distance. It was a phenomenal thing. The girl-child who had struggled in her education was back to where it all had begun, this time around staring poverty in the eye and telling it that she had defeated it.

Needless to say, I was very exhausted. I slept in my car on Sunday night, planning to travel back to Kampala on Monday morning after the ceremony. This was not a good decision. You see, I had not processed a leave of absence from work in order to attend these funeral rites; my plan was to use the weekend. I felt so convicted, being the HR implementer of policies, of being the one who broke them. I thought that I would have no moral authority telling employees at Total Uganda to do one thing while I myself did the exact opposite. To me, exemplary leadership is key. Therefore, I decided that I had to be back at the office on Tuesday as Monday was a public holiday, the Uganda independence anniversary.

As I had mentioned earlier, I normally work as if my entire life depends on it. In this case, that working as if my life depended on it nearly cost me my life and the lives of my son and my sisters and cousin. When I put my hands on my work, I do not spare anything in my power to make sure that all is done as per excellence and per standard. I am a great stickler for rules and regulations and always want to follow them to the letter.

In that occasion, the rules of the company stated that you could not take an annual leave without seeking prior approval from your supervisor. That was something that I had not done, and frankly, I must have overestimated my capacity to handle that packed weekend. I must have thought it was something that I just had to go in and get out.

I was totally wrong as I was just about to find out about three hours later after setting off from Katakwi. Those moments of decision can easily shape your destiny. There is a song that says, *"Live every moment leaving nothing to chance."* And on that occasion, I had left my entire life, plus the lives of four other people, including my son, to great risk by making the decision to drive under fatigue.

Much as my family pleaded with me to stay a little longer and have some rest, I wanted to be back in Kampala on time for work. Particularly my brother Samson pleaded with me to take some time and rest because I was visibly tired. I had been driving from Friday all the way from Kampala. In between, I had been running errands for the family the whole of Saturday, and I did not have enough time to rest and recuperate. And now, I was embarking on an even longer journey from Katakwi all the way to Kampala. It was understandable for Samson to be this concerned; anybody would.

On the other hand, a close relative was not in a talking mood with me. We had had our differences over the years because of a misunderstanding that was pegged all the way back when they chipped in so I could go to school. In fact, at that time, Sister Susan was fully aware of what was happening about my lack of school fees. When she heard about this benevolence, albeit in strained circumstances, she made a promise: "One day, we shall pay it back with the first salary that you will receive."

And ladies and gentlemen, that was exactly what happened. Not only did I have the opportunity to make it good for my relative as Sister Susan had prophesied, but I also purposed to start a business for them—I organized and paid all the expenses that they needed to incur in order to start a piggery business. We started by purchasing ten young piglets. In between, I offered support to their children by taking some of them to school.

However, somewhere down the line, the piggery business went south; I think he sold all the piglets. In between, they expected me to continue sending him money each month end. So they used to call me each month, expecting some money from me. One day, I put my foot down and flatly told them that I could not continue to do that. They were not any bit amused! They were enraged. "How could this lady do this to me when I was the one who helped educate her?" They were heard bitterly lamenting. At times, they would travel to Kampala and get to my house and cause all manner of disturbances.

Our relationship was totally ruined, probably beyond repair. But I would not be intimidated. So during the time that I was at home, we did not really see eye to eye with them. In fact, on the day that I would be traveling back, they were well aware but were nowhere to bid me goodbye.

Friends, such misunderstandings do happen in families. I think it can be normal because at some level, we expect our well-to-do siblings to have compassion on us and take care of us. We need to be careful here though. We cannot thrive on handouts. There is a massive difference between this close relative chipping in *for my school fees* and them getting monthly handouts from me. If I kept giving those to them, they would not develop. In my case, I had a project that I needed funding: schooling. As for this close relative, the money they demanded from me each month was not pegged to any project worth mentioning. I had already started a venture for them, and that would have been worth funding until it was self-sustaining. When I refused to continue funding them each month, it was a recipe for a broken relationship.

In my next book, I will be handling at length the topic of forgiveness and how crucial it has been in my life. There are very many people that I have had to forgive along my journey. Do not think it was easy to be abandoned by kith and kin in a place hundreds of kilometers away from home. If I had not dealt with that heartbreak, I would not be speaking to Uncle Nicholas, who was a very key person in my pursuit for education, today. He was the one who stoked the fire of my passion for education in the first place when he started educating me. Along the way, I also had to learn how to forgive other people, including those who, later on, were making fun of my speech impairment and my physical disability, conditions that I developed after escaping death, something that I am just about to share with you as I come to a close of the first part of my story.

Monday, October 9, 2006, will always be etched in my mind as long as I live. This is the day that marks the second part of my story. On the fateful day, we set off for Kampala after attending my parents' memorial service in my home village of Omukuny, Ongongoja Subcounty, in Katakwi District. In my car were my three-year-old son, Ronald; my immediate younger sister, Sarah Akiteng; and two of my cousins, Grace Akiteng and Sarah Amuge.

The day was very bright and shining with a lot of promise. Everyone in the vehicle was so excited about the journey. My sister sat at the codriver's seat, holding my son, while my cousin-sisters sat at the back seats. We set off immediately after breakfast, looking forward to be in Kampala later that afternoon. Two hours down the road, I stopped and texted a good friend and asked him to pray for me. I told him that I was driving back to Kampala, but I was feeling extremely tired.

As we proceeded, I caught myself dozing while driving several times. My passengers must also have dozed off because of the tiredness of the previous two days' activities. I decided that I would drive to the nearby center called Namutumba and get some well-needed rest before proceeding with the journey. That was about two hours or so after asking my friend to pray for me. As usual, I was putting on the full safety belt during the journey. Somewhere along the way, though, I felt so hot and restless. I decided to wear the safety belt half, just around my waist. I did this because I knew I was stopping just shortly after for a bit of rest.

Friends, I have had several near misses in my life. The latest near miss was the one when I could have graduated with first-class honors in social sciences from Makerere University. I missed it by decimals. According to Professor Epelu-Opio, if the university had considered my last two years only, it would not have been a problem to award me the first-class honors. My first year at Makerere was turbulent, and naturally, that impacted my performance. My first-year results affected the average score in the end.

I have had several near misses as an athlete, especially at the national level, because I did not have anybody to coach me. Every time I came in second or third, I was a very unhappy fellow, as is seen in one of my photos here. I think one of the greatest near misses for me was the one for the government scholarship to join Makerere University.

However, that time around, the near miss was close to fatal. Namutumba's trading center was within sight, just about 150 meters or so. But I caught myself dozing one last time, and that time, when I came to my senses, I was driving on the wrong side of the road. I do not remember much, but I must have been terribly frightened. In that fright, I must have stepped on the breaks harshly. The car lost control and rolled over several times before hitting a tree at the side of the road and coming to a halt. My son, Ronald, was thrown out of the car through the windshield and landed a few meters off. He fractured his leg and had a deep cut on his scalp. One of his ears was badly cut and just hung by a small thread, so to speak; it nearly came out. My sister also fractured her hand and had a deep laceration on her hand. The two cousin-sisters were the least injured as they just got bruises on them. Those of us who were at the front seat and the driver's seat were the ones who had bigger injuries.

Immediately after the accident happened, the local villagers swung into action, pillaging and robbing anything and everything that they could from the car. That was their main interest: things, not people! We were left for dead, or they must have thought that, from what they saw in the accident, we were already dead by the time the car hit the tree. I must have lost all consciousness on impact. However, I did not have any visible cuts on my body and was not bleeding anywhere. In fact, my injuries were not as physical as those of the others in the car. I never broke any part of my body apart from the neck.

Presently, a good Samaritan stopped by. He was driving his pickup truck. He had mercy on us, took us, and placed us in his pickup truck and was rushing us to the nearest hospital. This was about forty kilometers from the scene of the accident in Bugiri Hospital, Bugiri District. Once again, at the time when I was left for dead, another stranger was on hand to help me. This has been the story of my life. To date, I do not know where that gentleman is or what he is doing. I sure do hope to meet him someday. If anyone reading this knows how I can track him down, it will be of great importance to me.

A stranger found me years back while attempting to go to a police station to get recruited in the force. That stranger, wherever he is, shaped my life in a span of less than ten minutes. This stranger met us at our lowest point on that particular day. I have no idea what compelled him to help us the way he did, but he did it anyway. I believe that had he not helped us that day, probably the situation would have deteriorated very fast.

Across the globe, lives of different people are being altered forever and for the better by strangers who stop by and just do a random act of kindness. The currency for this kind of phenomenon is called compassion. I believe today that if people in the world we are living in will have more compassion for one another, great things will take place and lives will be changed in a major way. I believe that there are just two types of people on earth: those who are selfish and self-centered and those who are passionate and compassionate about others.

The selfish want to get all that they can get for themselves, and they will go to great lengths to put down others in their pursuit for things. I can easily make excuses for these kinds of people. Some treat life as a business transaction through and through. They tend to measure life by the mantra of "What is in it for me?" at all times in all things. I can say that some of them have seen abject poverty like the people at that trading center who robbed us clean instead of helping us at the scene of the accident. But then, there are people whose hearts are touched by the predicaments of others, and they go out of their way and their comfort zones to help others.

My brother who sold his cow did not know what kind of investment he was making, but I believe that his compassion played a major role in my life. My uncle Nicholas was touched with love and compassion as he watched me at my dad's graveyard, only a few years old. Three years earlier, before the death of my father, a relative had found my mom giving birth to me in our little hut and had compassion on us. Mom was unconscious, and I was on the floor. She could have turned aside and left us for the dead, but she did help. Sister Susan's mom could have embarked on a life of bitterness and revenge after her husband refused to take care of her. But she chose the high road of compassion for other people and, in the process, impacted the young girl Susan, who is helping very many girls as of this writing in 2016, to become a modern servant of God. It was compassion that caused Professor Epelu-Opio's secretary to get accommodation for me from her brother's hostel at least for one semester. It was also compassion that led my friend share with me her bed at Mary Stuart Hall in Makerere University. Friends, it was unrivaled compassion that made Professor Epelu-Opio to pledge and actually go ahead and pay for my tuition at Makerere University for two years. And if you talk to the humble professor today, you will realize that I was neither the first nor the last one that he helped.

Compassion is the driving force behind the work that Sister Susan is doing right now in Kenya. It is compassion that made the life of a boy called Mayanja be impacted by Sister Susan. There is a girl whose life is being impacted at the senior 6 level by the compassion of Sister Susan somewhere in Karamoja at the time of writing this. One of the former prominent leaders in Uganda was taught under the tutelage of Sister Susan. At the point of writing, there are several girls who are in the Parliament of Uganda as women representatives. They came straight from the hands of Sister Susan. There are many nurses in several hospitals, especially in Karamoja, who were once kids but were impacted by the works of Sister Susan.

My point is that with compassion, you may not have an idea of what difference you are making in the life of a single girl-child or, for that matter, any other human being in the face of the earth. But as the beneficiary of this phenomenon of compassion, I can tell you that sometimes, in situations of life and death, it is compassion that salvages the day.

Now, I know when I talk about compassion, many people think that it is something special that is only accomplished by avowed sisters and nuns. No, compassion is universal and one of the basic instincts of a human being. When you go to buy roasted maize by the roadside and see the woman roasting the maize holding her child in tattered clothes and see her distant gaze and deep thoughts, you are moved by compassion. One act of compassion is able to turn that life around.

Friends, I want to believe that the greatest achievements that the human race has gone through were acts of compassion, determination, and resilience. The bulb was not discovered because there was an abundance of resources. No, it was discovered because of the abundance of resilience. Your life can be the same, especially if you feel like you are giving up. The airplane was not invented because of an abundance of resources. It was invented because of passion. In fact, at the time of inventing the plane, it is reported that hundreds of thousands of dollars had been given in funding to a certain scholar to try to invent it, but it was preacher's sons who did it with less resources.

We read in the Bible that the heavens are paved with gold and other precious stones. Yet while coming on earth as an incarnate god, Jesus did not bring with him the gold and precious stones from heaven. His main currency was compassion, and today, he is the most influential person of all time since the world began.

There is so much to talk about my life. What I have shared with you is my story of resilience from the word *go*. But my story would never have been made complete without the contribution of many people, a great number of whom have been perfect strangers. This is what makes us humans as we are supposed to be. When we are faced with great odds, at times, all we need to do is to turn on the reserves within us, the reserves of determination, resilience, hope, and compassion, and continue forging and finding a way.

A few years back, the whole wide world watched as miners who had been trapped kilometers under the surface of the earth were being rescued. There was a collective sigh of relief as one miner after another was rescued against all the odds that they faced. Humans helping humans without needing to be paid for it—that is what it is all about.

A stranger in a pickup helping other strangers who had just had an accident—that is humanity at its best. Remember the day I was not miscarried after my mom fell off a roof while heavily pregnant with me? Remember how resilient I was when my mom was giving birth to me and passed out while alone in the homestead? Remember how I was traveling with Uncle Nicholas and the Karamojong warriors had just ambushed the car in front of us? Remember when they raided the school and killed a girl?

So it was that time around when I had that accident that I refused to die! Either that or God himself shielded and protected me all the while. As I come to the close of the first part of my story, my message is that we can do it. We can conquer poverty, and we can educate girl-children against all the odds that they face. We can do random acts of kindness all over the world, one person at a time. We do not necessarily have to wait for the United Nations, ChildFund, World Vision, Red Cross, and other organizations to start massive humanitarian drives. We can do this at our own backyards.

Today, you can make a telling difference in the life of a stranger. And as you do, sometimes you may feel like giving up. That is only natural. Sometimes you will come against terrible odds, and your first instinct will be to fend for yourself. But I challenge you to make it an intentional choice to make a difference in the life of a girl this year. You can visit any school and pay 300,000 Ugandan shillings for any girl who is having issues with school fees. I am telling you that we can do it.

Time does not allow me to tell the tale of how I got rescued from this terrible accident, but I can tell you that within twelve hours, I had lost my speech completely. I had been paralyzed on the right-hand side of my body. The loss of speech came in this wise: While at the hospital, they asked me to give them phone numbers of anybody that they could call. Off the top of my head, I gave them the numbers of my supervisor as well as a friend of mine. Later on, I overheard the nurses speaking on the phone and informing whomever they were calling about the condition of the survivors of the accident. She said, "The lady might survive, but the child might not make it." When I heard those words, I was traumatized, shocked, and terrified, and I immediately lost my speech.

One thing that I can tell you, though, is that one of the very first people to visit me at the hospital was the then managing director of Total Uganda, Mr. Christophe Jacquet. Although I could not talk to him by the virtue of my lost speech, I could hear him clearly. The words he said to me that day would be pivotal in the second part of my story, which I will be sharing in another book. He said, "Betty, I know you can hear me, and I want you to know that no matter what, we will wait for you."

Young Betty in Amudat in 1985

Betty's father Samson Icaarat in 1961
in Omukuny village, Ongongoja
Sub-county Katakwi District

Passport photo of Betty's
dad Samson Icaarat when
he was a sub-parish chief
in 1980 in Katakwi

Betty's mother

Betty picking cotton at the
SARI pathology department
in 1996 where she worked
for school fees during her
vacation in Serere district

Betty and the 3 people who played a crucial role
in her education, from Left to Right is Uncle
Nicholas B. Inyamit, Sister Susan Anyango,
Professor Justin Epelu-Opio in 2016 in Kampala

From Left to Right My brother Samson
Orukan, Betty Ogiel and Sister Susan
Anyango. Photo taken on the 5th
April, 2002 when I graduated from
Makerere University Kampala

Betty and a friend pumping
water for the school in
Kalungu GTC in 1997

Betty at the gate of Kangole
Girls during school holidays
when she stayed back at the
school to work for her welfare

Betty receiving her silver
medal for the 400 meters
race at the inter-university
games on the 24th Aprill 1999
held in Entebbe, Uganda

Betty receiving a certificate for outstanding performance in
the cross-country in Mukono on the 13th February in 1999

Betty after a training session
in Makerere University
Kampala in 1999

Betty in front the Makerere
University sports pavilion
where she resided for most the
time she was at the university

Betty at the Mabira Forest
during a Kalungu GTC
school study tour

Betty during a long relay
race at the inter-hall
athletics competition in
Makerere University

Made in the USA
Middletown, DE
10 April 2017